WOMEN
FIT TO
LEAD

Fernwood
Fitness partners

with founder **Diana Williams**

WOMEN
FIT TO
LEAD

**Females of Fernwood
Revolutionising Business**

First published in 2024 by Dean Publishing
PO Box 119
Mt. Macedon, Victoria, 3441
Australia
deanpublishing.com

DEAN PUBLISHING

Cataloguing-in-Publication Data
National Library of Australia
Title: Women Fit To Lead
Edition: 1st edition
ISBN: 978-1-925452-92-1
Category: Business & Entrepreneurship / Women in Business / Health

Contents

Diana
WILLIAMS

— INTRODUCTION —

FROM HUMBLE BEGINNINGS
TO FITNESS PHENOMENON

My journey began with a barbell in hand as I delved into weight training and powerlifting, discovering a transformative force that transcended physical boundaries. The longer I worked out with weights, the more I became convinced that this was a secret long kept from women about the amazing benefits that weight training had on our bodies and our minds. Weight training in gyms was a totally male-dominated domain. When I started weight training in that very blokey gym in Bendigo, I could not believe the changes it made to my physical shape, my emotional health, and, to my delight, my metabolism. I was sold on weight training for women, but I was in a minority. Most gyms – especially the weights areas in gyms – were not a place where many women felt comfortable. And to that point, neither did I. However, I knew John Clow, the owner of that gym, well, so I wasn't as intimidated as other women would have been.

He and I often talked about the idea of creating a gym for women, and the more we thought about it, the more it became a reality. We decided to form a partnership and start up a women's gym, which I would run, as he worked in a competitive gym on the other side of the city. I became focussed on a singular purpose: to create a sanctuary where women could embrace strength training, unshackled from societal norms. A place where we would have all the special little touches that women appreciate, but a serious weight training gym. When I look back on my journey, from being a stay-at-home mum, through to being a weightlifting enthusiast, and then becoming the visionary force behind Fernwood Fitness, it is quite amazing to me. However, my resilience, passion, and a fierce commitment to empowering women has taken this little business to the heights I never would have thought possible.

LITTLE GYM, BIG POTENTIAL

In 1989, fuelled by this fervour, I breathed life into the first Fernwood Fitness health club. The venue? A reclaimed classroom in the back streets of Bendigo, unassuming yet with heaps of possibility. Within those four walls, I didn't realise the potential at the time because I was just opening a little gym to introduce women to weight training. At that time, there were no thoughts of growing into a national brand, or even being a serious business. However, looking back on those days with my passion for wanting to make things better and being innovative and a doer rather than just a dreamer, this little gym in the back streets of Bendigo became the embryo of what we have now, a haven where women can defy stereotypes, lift weights, and discover their inner warriors, and an iconic Australian brand.

I guess my mission to dismantle the notion that weightlifting belonged solely to men was audacious. In an era when aerobics reigned supreme for women, I found it challenging to sell the concept to many women who felt that they would end up looking like bodybuilding poster girls. If only it were that easy. Men have testosterone and naturally more muscle. On the other hand, it takes a much greater amount of time and effort for women to build muscle, but the results can be spectacular. Who ever complained about having a lovely, lithe, toned body?

And so, the answer was Fernwood – a space where women could gather, sweat, and celebrate the joy of lifting. The name came from the idea of a space where women could come and take time out and be themselves with no expectations apart from improving their lives in a positive way.

The gym's dimensions may have been modest, but its impact was seismic. And my unwavering commitment attracted like-minded women who enjoyed the social and community aspect of what I had created as much as they enjoyed working out and the results they achieved. It didn't take long before my tiny little gym had to move to much larger premises in a more prominent part of the city, and from there it took off.

We had our logo, colours, and mission statement created through a Melbourne agency, had staff trained up and systems and process manuals created, and we were off on a journey that was not so much planned but driven by the demand for women to have their own space. The Fernwood movement of empowering women to shine took off, and there was no stopping us.

INSPIRING WOMEN TO FOLLOW THEIR DREAMS

From that reclaimed classroom, Fernwood Fitness has now blossomed and rippled across Australia, igniting a movement. Female franchise owners stepped forward, each a beacon of empowerment. Their stories have each woven into the fabric of Fernwood's legacy.

I am thrilled to introduce these amazing women in this book. They all have their own stories, their own challenges, their own strength, and, in many of them, some undiscovered strength that they never knew they had until they started a business and took on all of the challenges that come with that. Many of them have become businesswomen by default, as their husbands wanted good strong businesses that had a strong return on investment, but, as men cannot work directly in the business, their wives took on the roles of managing the day-to-day operations and have now discovered skills they never thought they had. Through them, we have empowered and enriched the lives of hundreds of thousands of Australian women. Our franchisees are women from all walks of life who have experienced the same pleasure as I have by coming to work in a space where every day we are thanked and appreciated by our members for creating this environment for them.

These women are strong, intelligent, commercially savvy businesswomen, and I applaud them for embarking on their own Fernwood journeys and, in turn, becoming role models to other women and young girls around the country. In doing so, they show them that if they follow their dreams, anything is possible, and the only thing standing in their way is themselves.

Through the strength of franchising, Fernwood has ignited the flame in so many women who may not have gone down the path of being businesswomen if it were not for Fernwood. It makes me proud to see them displaying their business acumen to new, incoming franchisees who are just starting to embark on their journeys. One of the greatest things about women in business is that we are willing to share and to mentor others and help them on their own journeys into the business world.

And so, the heartbeat of Fernwood Fitness thrives – a symphony of weights clanging, laughter echoing, and women rising. Fernwood isn't just a gym; it's a sisterhood, a place where women reclaim their strength, rewrite their stories, and forge bonds that endure.

I hope you enjoy reading the stories of these women and in some ways are inspired to follow your own dreams.

Di William

Di would love to share more with you about our amazing brand and her own Fernwood journey. Scan the QR code or follow the link to watch a personal video from Diana Williams.

SCAN ME

www.fernwoodfitness.com.au/womenfittolead

I PUT A LOT OF MY SUCCESS DOWN TO RADICAL

action and zero procrastination.

Melissa
JONES

BE THE BEST YOU CAN BE

My parents were both extremely resilient people who navigated hardship with the mentality that there was always a way. My father could figure out how to do things he had no training or expertise in. For example, he wasn't a fencer, but he could build a fence. He wasn't a builder, but he could build a veranda. He had a work ethic like no one else I knew. My mother, to say it lightly, believed in me wholeheartedly and convinced me I could do whatever I wanted in life. I once asked her how she would feel if I became a garbage truck driver, and her answer was simple – "I would be proud if you were the best garbage truck driver you could be." It doesn't matter what you do with your life, as long as you do your best.

At the ripe old age of 23, I applied for a club manager position at the company-owned Fernwood in Penrith – and

I got the job! It was the highest position I had held in my relatively young career. Suddenly, I was managing a group of women, many 20–30 years my senior. Walking into the club as their new manager was daunting. I needed to get them onside and have them buy into my vision of creating a better culture and providing better services for our members. It was an extremely difficult task, and I was met with constant pushback.

After my first Fernwood conference and nine months into managing the club, I contacted Di and then-CFO Eric to purchase the club. I could see that I was making waves of positive change, and I knew how much potential the club had. Di is an inspiring woman, starting Fernwood in her 40s after she had already had children. She has proven to so many women that it's never too late to follow your dream or start a new career. At the time, I definitely needed some inspiration.

With no money, living with my parents, $10,000 of personal loan debt, and no idea how I was going to purchase the club, I still made that phone call, deciding I would figure out the logistics later. Somehow, I made it work, and, in 2015, I became the owner of Fernwood Penrith at only 24 years old.

THE REALITY OF LEADERSHIP

The day I took over the club, I had meetings with each staff member to explain that I had purchased the business and their employment would be with me instead of head office, if they wished to stay. One by one, half of my staff resigned, many of them telling me I wouldn't make it as a club owner. They believed I was turning their gym into a 'teeny-bopper' facility, and they wanted no part of it. "You won't last a year," some of them declared.

I'm so thankful they shared their opinions because it lit a fire in me to prove them wrong, and, more than eight years later, I'm still here, more successful than ever, helping women in our local community be the best versions of themselves.

As a leader, I've learnt to trust my gut. There have been so many times when I haven't listened to my gut, and it has always backfired. I also believe that self-development is important. In a business, success starts and finishes with the leader and their team. Without strength of mind, you won't succeed. You need to build yourself up for the challenges ahead.

For years, as a club owner, I underpaid myself so I could pay my team more, which led to feelings of resentment. I was the one who took on all the risk and worked long hours – why shouldn't I earn a fair salary? Now I pay myself according to my worth, which is something all business owners should do when they can.

I put a lot of my success down to radical action and zero procrastination. I believe in making a decision and moving forward, even if you're wrong, because then you can learn, as opposed to sitting and doing nothing, which can only result in nothing.

MERGING WORK AND LIFE

Three months after purchasing the club, already feeling over-whelmed, I found out I was pregnant (surprise!). At the time, I didn't believe I could have it all – career, family, financial stability – however, my husband and I made it work.

Often, I would take work home and take family to work. It's how I've managed to maintain a work-life balance – by mixing work and life. I've breastfed my babies while paying invoices at home, and I've sat in conferences while rocking my babies to sleep. I've tried to be the best mother and business owner I can be.

As far as exercise goes, I just do what I can when I can. When I set very specific goals, like running a marathon, I tend to stick to my training. However, during periods of heavy work, I may only work out once a week. When the club is quieter, I may find myself working out six times a week. Whatever's happening in my life, I just roll with it, and I don't let myself feel guilty. I'm doing the best I can.

Fortunately, as a brand, Fernwood aligns with my core values, which means I love my job, and I never wake up on a Monday morning dreading the work week. I'm always excited to be in the club, and I don't see that changing anytime soon.

Keirsten WALLACE

— MORNINGTON, VICTORIA —

OUR CLUB IS A COMMUNITY

When I became a member of Fernwood Mitcham, I instantly felt comfortable and supported by the other members and staff. It was the only gym where I'd had that experience. I loved that it was women-only, and I never felt intimidated or worried about what I was wearing, how I looked, or what I was doing. Gradually, I gained confidence in classes and started working with a personal trainer. It was the best decision I ever made, and I developed a true love for the brand and everything it stood for.

I, along with my husband Anthony, had been talking about buying a franchise for a while, but the right opportunity hadn't come along – yet. When an admin assistant position came up at the Mitcham club, I applied immediately, determined to get the job, get a feel for what it was like to work for Fernwood, and see how the back end of the business functioned.

I loved it so much that I quickly began the process of applying to become a franchisee. During the application process, I met Di for the first time. She's a true visionary and someone I've always looked up to. I admire the business she has created and the communities that form within all the Fernwood clubs across the country. As a person, she's personable and friendly, while also being a shrewd businesswoman. It was wonderful to meet such an empowering female leader who has built such a successful franchise.

Fernwood Mornington was the second club we looked at, and we saw a lot of potential there. I planned to approach running the club from more of a member's perspective and create the community feel I experienced at Mitcham – and that's exactly what I did.

FAKING IT, THEN MAKING IT

When I took over Fernwood Mornington, I had no experience running a club. It may sound like a cliché, but 'fake it till you make it' can be good advice. It's surprising what you can bluff your way through when you're polite, helpful, and willing to listen to people's needs. You won't always have the answers, and that's fine. Sometimes, getting the right answer takes time and research. It's okay to say, "I'm not sure, let me get back to you." Often, members just want to be heard, acknowledged, and respected. Member satisfaction is very important to me, and I always strive for the highest level of cleanliness and service in my club.

From the beginning, I loved being my own boss and having flexibility with the hours I worked in the club. So much can be done from home, but spending time in the club is very important to me, and I'm there at least four days a week.

When you own a business, you're on pretty much all the time, but I've learnt it's important to take some time out and switch off when you can. In my experience, it will help clear your head and make you more productive when you are working. When I first took over the club, my three children were still quite young – 9, 11, and 13 – and running the business took up more time than I anticipated, but we made it work. For example, during school holidays, the kids would come into the club and find little jobs to do to keep them occupied. They actually loved it!

Over time, I've built a strong team, which has allowed me to have much more flexibility with my schedule. I've now (mostly) stopped answering emails and working from home after hours. I also make sure the family eats together at the table every night, and we have a 'no laptops after dinner' rule. Maintaining an exercise routine is also important, and I love getting out for a walk in nature on the weekends. Really, I try to get outside most days, as it helps me stay grounded. My schedule can get quite busy, and I find that booking a PT (personal training) session 2–3 times a week keeps me accountable. I can't make excuses if I have a session booked. I also participate in reformer Pilates, which adds a nice balance to my routine.

As far as my diet goes, I like the 80/20 rule. What do I mean? I eat clean and exercise most days – about 80 percent of the time – but I allow myself to indulge now and again without feeling guilty.

Working hard is important, but so is making time for yourself. To be a good leader, you must keep yourself physically and mentally healthy.

AN HONEST MISTAKE

In business, you will make mistakes, some big, some small, and some, honestly, can be quite amusing.

Prior to the club switching to 24/7, we would close at the end of the day. One Saturday afternoon, I was ready to close up, so I checked to make sure everyone had left. As far as I could tell, I was alone in the club. At the time, we had a massage chair in a separate room. When I walked past, the door was closed, and I had no reason to believe anyone was in there, so I left the building and began locking the front door.

To my surprise, a member came running towards the door, yelling. She had been in the massage chair, and I almost locked her in the club. Luckily, she found the situation funny, and we had a good laugh. To this day, we still joke about that time she almost got locked in the club for the weekend.

OUR MEMBERS – THE LIFEBLOOD OF THE CLUB

Even when I'm busy focusing on the big-picture aspects of running the club, I always try to interact with our members as much as possible. If I'm in the club, I usually spend some time on reception or on the gym floor. It's important for members to see me there, and some like to stop for a chat, which I always enjoy. It's all about maintaining the community aspect of the club that first compelled me to join the franchise.

So many of our members are true inspirations to us all. Some have a lot of health issues and struggle with their weight. But guess what? They're constantly in the club, working out, doing FIIT30, personal training, and more. They keep coming back because there's no prejudice, no judgement, no criticism. Everyone treats them like the beautiful, inspirational people they are. It's what we're all about.

OCCASIONALLY, A MEMBER WILL TELL US THAT WE NOT ONLY CHANGED HER LIFE BUT *saved it too,* WHICH IS TRULY HUMBLING TO HEAR

Donna LEE

A LOVE OF SMALL BUSINESS

After earning my personal trainer (PT) qualification, I began looking for work that would line up with my family commitments. As a single mum, I could only work during school hours, so I applied for a PT position at my local Fernwood club in Tuggeranong and got the job.

Instantly, I felt an amazing energy within the club. Within two weeks, I knew I wanted to do more, so I approached the owner and offered to buy the club. Eighteen months later, in 2011, I, along with another lady who worked at the club, became a co-owner of Fernwood Tuggeranong.

BEYOND LIFE-CHANGING

My business partner had plenty of gym sales experience, and I had a background in small business, which made us the perfect team. I bought my first small business, a childcare centre, at age 23 and ran it for 12 years, selling it before commencing study to become a PT. Together, my business partner and I turned a great club into a thriving business, winning club of the year several times.

As a franchisee, I got to know Di Williams as an amazing lady who is always working to stay ahead in the fitness industry. She's the reason why we've managed to remain one of Australia's leading fitness franchises for so many years.

However, the best thing about running a Fernwood club is knowing we're having a huge positive impact not only on our members but also on our team. That impact then ripples through the community to their families, children, and friends. To me, it's not just a job. It's not just a business. Ultimately, we're changing lives in a really positive way.

Occasionally, a member will tell us that we not only changed her life but saved it too, which is truly humbling to hear. Frequently, members tell us how much happier they've been since joining the club. It's like a second home to them. They feel comfortable, and so many of our members who've met at the club have become best friends.

A SHARED PASSION

Looking back, my dad played a major role in shaping who I am today. He was a small business owner with a great work ethic and a love of small business, two traits I quickly adopted.

One of his mottos was: "Do it once, do it well." It's a sentiment I bring to any task I undertake today. I'm a big believer in positive thinking. What you think is what you get. Another powerful belief I inherited from Dad was: "If you can dream it, you can make it happen." I truly believe this. Why? Because I've lived it.

Over the years, I've learnt that the keys to running a successful small business are to offer amazing customer service and create a great work environment. If you can nail these two elements, the rest will come much easier. It's the secret to my club's ongoing success.

AROUND EVERY CORNER IS A NEW

experience,

A NEW

lesson,

A NEW NUGGET OF

wisdom.

Alexa & Mick
DOWLING

AN UNBEATABLE PARTNERSHIP

I'd like to say the idea to open a women-only gym was mine, but it wasn't. My male partner, Michael, gets all the credit. Who would've thought he had that inner woman in him all this time? His idea completely changed the trajectory of our lives – for the better!

Previously, Michael and I both worked government jobs, living on the Sunshine Coast. Michael was a detective with the Queensland Police Service, and I was a social worker, working for the Department of Families. While we both had fulfilling careers, we were always on the lookout for new opportunities. Michael is very entrepreneurial, and, more than anything, he wanted to run his own business.

In 2001, the opportunity came up to buy an Eagle Boys franchise in Brisbane, which would mean uprooting our entire lives to live in a different part of the state. After much consideration, we went ahead with the move – new house, new city, new job for me, while Michael trained to be a franchisee. It was an extremely stressful time. Even our dog, Bubba, was unhappy. He hated Brisbane.

To help deal with the stress, I decided I needed to exercise, so I signed up at Fernwood Fitness Carindale. In the welcome pack, there was a book Di had written about the beginning of the Fernwood franchise. I couldn't put it down – it was amazing.

Michael decided not to go ahead with Eagle Boys and began looking for other business opportunities. One day, while sitting at the kitchen table, contemplating his options, he picked up my Fernwood membership card, which I'd left sitting on the table. When I got home, he asked me about the business. What could I say? I gave him the book. "You've got to read this," I said. "The people who started Fernwood are amazing." After some research, Michael decided that he loved the concept, and we submitted an application to become franchisees.

NO EXPERIENCE? NO WORRIES!

When we met Di and John at Fernwood Carindale in November 2000, we couldn't believe how normal and down-to-earth they were. I tried my best to come off as professional and knowledge-able, but, understandably, I had some self-doubt. What could a social worker possibly know about running a gym? However, Di instantly put me at ease with her humility, professionalism, and authenticity. She clearly hadn't let fame and fortune go to her head. With no business experience, no experience in the fitness industry, and very little capital, we were approved.

After inspecting a potential site in a Morayfield shopping centre, we agreed we had found the perfect space for our first Fernwood Fitness club. As a bonus, we could move back to the Sunshine Coast, which made us all, especially Bubba, very happy. So, in March 2002, we moved back to the Sunny Coast to open our club.

Who would start a business from the ground up, from fit-out to doors open, with absolutely no idea what they were doing? We would! Michael and I had no experience with fit-outs, sales, or running a business in general, so it was very much a 'learn as you go' situation. All I can say is thank God for Mark Brown, the general manager – we couldn't have done it without him.

NEW BUSINESS, NEW CHALLENGES

Due to our previous occupations, what we lacked in business experience, we made up for in customer service skills. I truly believe our commitment to high-level service helped us survive those first couple of years.

Customer service is always our number one priority. When we first opened our doors, a big challenge was learning to manage staff in a way that allowed us to offer the high level of service we strived for. We believe that, despite what's happening in the business or our own lives, we must always show up with smiles on our faces and be totally present every single day. As far as we're concerned, the customer is always right – even when they're wrong.

Over time, we managed to overcome most of our earlier challenges, but we've learnt that we can never be complacent.

Just when you think you've got everything figured out – bam! A new problem comes right out of left field. In business, we realised early on that you must learn to be vigilant, adaptable, and resilient; otherwise, the next challenge could be the one that takes you out of the game for good.

One challenge we're yet to fully overcome is working together as a couple. It takes effort to ensure that disagreements about the business don't become arguments within the marriage. Michael is a typical Leo, meaning he wants to call all the shots and doesn't like getting caught up in the details. I, on the other hand, am more detail-oriented and like to do everything by the book. As you can imagine, our contrasting personalities make for some interesting discussions and outcomes.

STAYING AHEAD OF THE GAME

Our most pivotal moments in business always come from Michael. While he has had many grand ideas over the years, his biggest and most impactful came to him one night while he was having a beer.

"What do you think about opening the club twenty-four seven?" he said. I don't recall my exact response, but I do remember thinking it would mean more work for me. Regardless, I sat down at the computer and typed a proposal for Di. She may not have appreciated all the Harley Davidson analogies – things like, Fernwood, like Harley Davidson, isn't just a brand but a cultural icon and lifestyle – but she did agree that we should pilot the idea. So, on 9 August 2012, we became the first 24/7 Fernwood Fitness club, and, as they say, the rest was history. Michael's big idea paid off, even if it meant he could no longer work out at the club after hours, which was one of the perks of owning a gym. The operational, reputational, and membership benefits to our club were immense and continue to this day. Best idea ever, Michael! Our success at Morayfield enabled us to buy our own premises at Noosa and open up our second Fernwood club.

We're always looking for new ways to innovate and stay ahead of the game. Michael is constantly researching, not just topics related to the fitness industry but also anything that might impact the economy domestically or internationally. His commitment to research is one of the reasons why many of the concepts and processes we've implemented have been so successful. He believes that, to stay relevant and ahead of the competition, you must be on your game and know exactly what's going on around you. If there's a new innovation in the fitness industry, he'll know about it. He's always on the lookout for the next big thing. Not every concept is a roaring success like the idea to switch to 24/7 – you win some; you lose some – but at least we're always moving forward, one way or another.

LEARNING IS A CONTINUOUS PROCESS

In business, you will make mistakes. You will make bad decisions. You will fail. But that's okay. In fact, it's a part of the process. If Michael and I had $1 for every mistake we made, we would be billionaires ten times over.

Having said that, I'm a big believer that we should learn from our mistakes and if we don't, we deserve what we get. Harsh, I know, but our failures are gifts, and we shouldn't squander them. To be successful, we must learn from every misstep and make better future decisions.

Even though we've been in business for over two decades, we don't know it all. We can't know it all. Around every corner is a new experience, a new lesson, a new nugget of wisdom. The key is to be open to receiving them.

Marita SMITH

WHEN A PASSION BECOMES A CAREER

My narrative, spanning 24 years from Lima, Peru to my tenure at Fernwood in Australia, is a tapestry woven with passion, trials, and an unyielding pursuit of dreams.

Growing up in Lima, I immersed myself in athletics, as well as representing my school in volleyball. In year 9, through a twist of fate, the athletics coach observed me sprinting from class to the volleyball court and invited me to participate in athletics trials. Selected for the sprinting team, I discovered a profound passion for sports, though the last year of school introduced me to the bittersweet taste of defeat against taller opponents.

Despite excelling in mathematics, I deviated from the expected engineering path, which disappointed my father, leading to my parents pushing me into the corporate world, where I worked as an executive bilingual secretary for one year before deciding to break free. My decision, while it concerned my parents, led me to stumble upon my true calling – fitness, particularly step aerobics.

Life took another unexpected turn when my parents nudged me towards a four-year IT course. I also delved into marketing, working for a prominent Peruvian beer company. During this time, fitness competitions and group workouts became my sanctuary, and, gradually, I found myself transitioning into instructing aerobics.

I eventually bought into a partnership in the gym where I trained. It was a bodybuilding gym, and the owner wanted to attract more women. In an 85 percent male gym, I played multiple roles: outreach, reception, cleaning, running fat burner and step classes. The camaraderie with the team of eight men provided a memorable experience, and I enjoyed learning more about training and nutrition. In my mind, there was no doubt that I had found my calling in the fitness industry.

A TWIST OF FATE

Amid personal upheavals, including a breakup with my long-term boyfriend, fortune intervened when I met my now-husband Scott, who was travelling in Peru. Eventually, he asked me to accompany him back to Australia. Could I give up the familiarity of my home country to step into the unknown? I was filled with uncertainty and doubt. When my Australian tourist visa was denied, I took it as a sign that I should stay in Peru. However, Scott managed to resolve the issue, and, with only a few days' notice, I sold my portion of the gym, said goodbye to my friends, and boarded a plane to Brisbane.

In October 2000, when I landed in Australia, I was captivated by the sunny, green landscapes of Brisbane. Scott, aware of my devotion to fitness, got me a year's membership at a new gym named Zest in the Carindale shopping centre. However, the opening was delayed by several months, which led to me joining Fernwood Carindale as a casual member. Here, I was introduced to Les Mills classes, a concept unfamiliar in my home country where everything was freestyle.

Fernwood Carindale became my haven. Scott persuaded me to obtain fitness instructor registration so I could teach a few classes per week to provide me with a purpose. Although hesitant due to my strong accent and English being a second language, I agreed to undertake the course.

With the launch of Les Mills' Body Jam in Australia, I saw an opportunity for me to become an instructor, but sponsorship from a gym was a prerequisite. A fortuitous trip to watch my husband play squash led to a meeting with Lea-Anne, the trainer teaching the Body Jam course, which facilitated my inclusion. In the course, I defied the odds by being 1 of only 2 out of 15 participants who passed.

Armed with my registration, I found myself taking over from the regular Body Jam instructor at Zest, doing classes for free, as she wasn't familiar with the new releases. Fernwood Carindale's group fitness coordinator noticed, leading to a trial class at Fernwood that marked the beginning of my paid classes in Australia.

My background in freestyle classes led me to diversify, gaining confidence to teach Body Step, Body Pump, Body Combat, and a variety of freestyle classes. The popularity of

Fat Burner and Step soared as I incorporated dance movements into my routines.

As I didn't have a driver's licence, teaching fill-in classes initially required Scott to chauffeur me. Once I did get my licence, my unfamiliarity with Brisbane's roads led to numerous calls to my husband for help, as I would frequently get lost. As my reputation grew, offers for back-to-back classes poured in, which made the travel more manageable. What began as a part-time hobby became a commitment of 27 classes per week.

The revelation of my pregnancy prompted me to explore Pilates, a decision driven by uncertainty around my ability to continue high-impact routines. Despite initial challenges and confusion during the Pilates course, I persevered, eventually mastering the fundamentals through self-learning and practice.

With the demand for Pilates classes soaring, self-learning became a necessity. Offers flooded in, and I found myself juggling multiple classes, earning substantially more, and receiving requests for back-to-back sessions.

Participating in gym openings, including Fernwood Loganholme, Fitness First Mt Gravatt, and Goodlife Holland Park, cemented my reputation in the industry. Fernwood Carindale and Fernwood Loganholme emerged as my preferred gyms, providing a sense of appreciation and acknowledgment that fuelled my ambition to one day own a gym myself.

SEIZING OPPORTUNITY

When Fernwood Loganholme came up for sale, I thought I had found my pathway to club ownership. However, devastation struck when the club was sold before I had a chance to make an offer. Fortunately, fate had another plan.

When Fernwood Underwood went on the market, I seized the opportunity. I was four months pregnant at the time, so, initially, I don't think anyone thought I was serious about the purchase. However, with Scott's backing, I began the application process. To get familiar with the members and the business, I worked in the club for a couple of months. During this time, I began planning for the challenge of balancing a newborn with a new business.

After several trips to Melbourne to meet Di and the team, I officially became the proud owner of Fernwood Underwood.

MY CLUB IS MORE THAN A BUSINESS

Owning a gym came with a whole new set of challenges, from knocking down walls to expand the creche to navigating the complexities of personal training leadership.

One day, during the early years of running the club, I left my 2-year-old son in my office, and he somehow managed to lock the door. We couldn't find the key, so I, a desperate mother in a female-only gym, got a ladder and climbed into the roof to try and rescue him. The problem was, no one told me I had to stay on the rafters, and I came crashing through the ceiling, unfortunately still outside the office. At this point, one of my staff members went next door and found a man to help us. In the end, he rescued my son, and I only ended up with a few cuts and bruises.

Immediately, Fernwood Underwood became more than a business; it became a passion, a place filled with sweat, screams, laughter, and enduring friendships. Despite the exhausting schedule, the purpose derived from helping our members improve their lives uplifts me. If I didn't own a Fernwood gym, I would still be one of the brand's top ambassadors.

Reflecting on my journey, I've had to overcome many hurdles in Australia, including mastering a new language and dealing with hostility from others for being an outsider. Ultimately, succeeding in the industry I love required perseverance and determination, but I got there in the end.

Fernwood stands out as one of the best chapters of my Australian life. It was the first gym that offered me a job, treating me with respect despite my cheeky accent. Looking ahead, I cannot envision myself being anywhere else.

Guneet
CHEEMA

WOMEN CAN HAVE IT ALL

I began my Fernwood journey as a member, an experience that made me fall in love with the brand. In every Fernwood club, there's a genuine care factor and community feel that sets them apart in a highly competitive industry.

I've always admired women who can balance work and family. If I'm pursuing my goals, I'm at my best. I'm happy, fulfilled, and I don't feel like I'm making sacrifices. By pursuing my dreams, I'm showing my kids how to pursue theirs.

For women, financial independence is important, as a financially independent woman can live life on her terms – it's the best advice I got from my mum. To gain my own financial independence, I always wanted to have my own business, which I could run my way, but it had to be a business that resonated with me, one that I could grow with skill and hard work, fulfilling my dream of becoming a successful businesswoman.

Due to my personal experience with the Fernwood brand, becoming a club owner felt right, so, when the opportunity arose, I chose to be the girl who went for it.

A REWARDING EXPERIENCE

I first met Di in 2007. I was very nervous before our meeting, but, within a couple of minutes, she made me feel so comfortable. For such an amazing businesswoman, she's so humble, grounded, and approachable. She's an absolute inspiration to young businesswomen like me. She has been so supportive throughout my journey, playing a big part in my success over the years. She shows young aspiring businesswomen how it's done, and, for that, she's my idol.

As a club owner, it's so rewarding to see women achieve their health and fitness goals. The club often becomes a second home to our members, and they love being a part of such a vibrant and supportive community. The brand has managed to reach many women who were shy or felt too intimidated to join a gym, and it's so rewarding to see their confidence grow, feeling comfortable and supported in the club as they achieve their goals.

YOU CAN ACHIEVE ANYTHING

For me, owning a club has meant exponential learning and growth. I didn't fully understand my potential as a business owner until I bought the club and found my passion.

I'm very ambitious, and Fernwood has certainly brought out the best in me. To stay on top of my workload, I write out all of my daily, weekly, and monthly tasks. That way, I know exactly what I need to do and when. I also set weekly, monthly, and quarterly goals for myself – both professional and personal – and for my clubs. Once the goals are set, I then create an action plan to achieve them.

You should always have a clear vision for your business so you and your team know what you're working towards. The key is to set both short- and long-term goals, create an action plan to achieve them, and track your progress over time – daily, weekly, monthly, quarterly, and yearly.

Of course, running a successful business takes time and effort. To maintain a healthy work-life balance, I have a very structured routine, sleeping, training, working, and eating at the same time every day. Having such a rigid structure helps me fit everything into my schedule. As club owners, it's important to practise what we preach and show women how we can play different roles and still focus on our health and fitness. It's so important to look after yourself, as you can't pour from an empty cup. If you're not looking after yourself first, how can you be at your best to help others?

In my life, I've learnt that where there's a will, there's a way. If you want it, you can make it work, one way or another. As women, we can have it all, and I try my best to live this every day. To realise your dreams, you must push yourself out of your comfort zone. Trust your gut, believe in yourself, and then go for it. You can achieve anything you set your mind to.

FOR ME,
WORK ISN'T JUST
A MEANS TO
MAKE A LIVING;
it's a source
OF JOY AND
FULFILMENT.

Renee
ZAMMIT

EMPOWERING WOMEN TO ACHIEVE THE IMPOSSIBLE

In 2006, I embarked on my Fernwood journey as a personal trainer (PT) in Loganholme, Queensland. After relocating to the central coast of New South Wales, I transitioned to the Hornsby club as a food coach. Eventually, I found my niche at Fernwood Penrith, working as a personal trainer for approximately four years. Within a couple of years, I had assumed the role of head PT, and I revelled in the opportunity to build a robust client base and empower women to achieve what they once deemed impossible. Despite my passion, life circumstances led me to step away from the industry for seven years.

By the time my husband and I moved to Burleigh on the Gold Coast, I was eager to re-enter the fitness realm. I sought part-time opportunities, eventually landing at Fernwood Robina.

Beginning on reception, I navigated the challenges of the pandemic and eventually assumed the position of club coordinator. Three years later, the stars aligned, and, in July 2023, my husband and I proudly became the new owners of Fernwood Robina.

MY TEAM IS MY STRENGTH

My husband and I had a pre-planned four-week holiday scheduled shortly after we took over the club. Thus, within just three weeks of becoming the owners, we embarked on a month-long overseas journey. I was incredibly fortunate to have an exceptionally supportive team that capably managed the club during my absence, leaving me with no concerns. It might not have been the right time, but it was definitely the right decision.

From the outset, I've treated my staff with respect, and they always come through for me. This approach fosters open communication and collaboration, resulting in a cohesive and motivated team. Together, we've created a positive work environment that promotes morale and productivity. It's a warm and welcoming atmosphere, a place where women connect, lift each other up, and celebrate their successes together. Ultimately, recognising and prioritising employee wellbeing reduces turnover, which contributes to long-term success. In the end, everyone wins.

CHOOSE A JOB YOU LOVE, AND YOU WILL NEVER WORK A DAY IN YOUR LIFE

The idea of doing something I love for work has been my compass for navigating my career path. To me, it's important to recognise the value of aligning my career with my passions.

By choosing a job that aligns with my interests and values, I've experienced a shift in my attitude towards work. For me, work isn't just a means to make a living; it's a source of joy and fulfilment. I've dedicated myself to exploring and embracing my true passions, ensuring that every day feels like a rewarding journey rather than a mundane task. I feel empowered to make informed career choices, transforming my work into a meaningful and purposeful endeavour. It's not just about finding a job; it's about crafting a career that brings genuine happiness and a sense of purpose to my life.

I'm fortunate to truly love what I do, so it never feels like work.

MY SECOND HOME

The fitness industry has always held a special place in my heart, and Fernwood feels like a second home. When the opportunity arose to become a franchisee, it felt like the ideal fit.

When I first encountered Di in the Robina club in 2022, she undeniably lived up to my expectations. I had heard numerous commendable things about her over the years and when I saw it all in person, it solidified my love for the amazing brand she has built. At that point, the decision to become a franchisee was simple.

As a club owner, it's fulfilling to see the positive changes and the feelings of strength and confidence grow among our members, which motivates me to keep working towards supporting women's health and happiness. Fernwood Robina isn't just a gym; it's a community hub where our fantastic team plays a crucial role in creating a positive and empowering environment for every member.

In my career, I've learnt to always embrace change. I remain open to experimenting with new strategies and consistently seeking ways to enhance our products, services, and processes. Adapting to the evolving needs of the market is crucial to ensure the business stays competitive and resilient now and into the future. As a club owner, the work never stops, and I wouldn't have it any other way.

Mel
ROBINSON

MAKING IT ON MY OWN

After graduating with a Bachelor of Arts (double major in communication and psychology), I realised that I wasn't interested in working in those fields. So, in my early 20s, while working in part-time administration roles, I enrolled in a Bachelor of Accounting and eventually went to work for Queensland Health.

I was ambitious, worked hard, and managed to progress quickly up the public service ladder. I started out in the finance department and then moved into health funding policy. For the most part, I worked in a corporate environment, writing funding policies, cabinet submissions, and briefs requesting funding for public health services. While I enjoyed the work, my dream was to own my own business. Be my own boss. Set my own hours. See if I could make it on my own.

After 12 years with the Queensland Public Service, I knew it was time to move on, and I started looking at businesses to purchase. Initially, I considered buying a coffee shop; however, it felt like I would be taking on more risk for less money than I would if I just continued with Queensland Health. Also, the hours weren't great; staff turnover was high, and profit per sale was low. Next, I looked at a newsagency, but I felt that I would get bored quite quickly. Finally, I stumbled upon the listing for Fernwood Fitness Browns Plains.

I liked the idea of working in a space that empowered women, and the numbers seemed to stack up. I had an external accountant review the books and got the green light to go ahead with the purchase, so I pressed on and bought the club. On 20 June 2008, I officially became the owner of Fernwood Fitness Browns Plains. It was both exciting and nerve-racking. Honestly, I had no idea what I was in for.

A SERIES OF TOUGH LESSONS

After purchasing my first club, I quickly realised that I spoke a corporate and public service language, which wasn't how people spoke in the fitness industry. Consequently, I struggled to connect with sales staff, group fitness instructors, and personal trainers. As it turned out, being good at writing funding submissions didn't translate to being good at running a gym. Combine my inability to effectively communicate with my team with the global financial crisis and a lack of sales experience, and the first few years of business were incredibly difficult.

Over time, my membership numbers dropped, and we were making little to no profit. Initially, I struggled to accept that running a gym involves two key areas: fitness *and* sales. Fitness is reasonably easy to get right. It's sales that can be a problem when you don't understand the criticality of sales management, which I didn't at the time. I certainly learnt that one the hard way.

To save my sinking club, I took advantage of sales management training seminars and hired people who understood what sales for Fernwood was all about: inspiring women to prioritise their health and fitness. Gradually, our sales improved, and membership numbers increased. Finally, I began to feel like I could make the business a success. Little did I know that even tougher times were on the horizon.

FACED WITH A DIFFICULT DECISION

In 2010 and 2011, Brisbane experienced a number of wild storms. While the industrial area around us had undergone a lot of development, the council hadn't kept up with the required infrastructure, and, on three occasions, the club floor completely flooded.

Fortunately, our equipment wasn't damaged; however, the insurance company declined further insurance unless the cause of flooding was addressed. The landlord wouldn't accept responsibility, which brought us to an impasse. Eventually, we decided to relocate, losing a $36,000 rental bond in the process. The bank almost didn't back the move. It was a very stressful time.

In September 2011, we opened the doors to our beautiful, newly relocated club, complete with a modernised Fernwood fit-out. It was absolutely the best, and bravest, decision I had ever made, and I don't regret it for a second.

THE NEXT SET OF CHALLENGES

In 2016, I separated from my husband of almost 17 years. It was a difficult divorce, but, in the end, I managed to keep the gym and my partially renovated house, starting a new chapter as a sole business owner, single mother, and house renovator, with two children in private school.

To support my children during this time, I had no choice but to spend less time in the club. I had to relinquish some control and empower the staff to step up. To their absolute credit, they did, and, in that, I learnt another valuable life lesson. To be a good leader, you don't have to hold the reins too tightly. Setting the direction, sharing your vision, and truly valuing your employees is business gold.

The next big challenge was the COVID pandemic. It was terrifying. I literally had no income and no idea if I would lose the business. As a brand, we had built strong communities within our clubs, which helped enormously to pull us through. We were fortunate that, in Queensland, our closures were shorter than our counterparts in New South Wales and Victoria. Since COVID, my club and our brand have come back so much stronger, and our members value our in-club community more than ever.

AN ENTICING OPPORTUNITY

In late 2022, Di presented me with the opportunity to purchase the Loganholme club. I had always wanted to be a multi-site franchisee. In fact, I had already purchased the rights to open a club in Springfield Lakes whenever the right site came up. I was even in the process of building a house five minutes from Springfield so I could live in the community when I opened the new club! At that stage, I hadn't planned to purchase another club, but the opportunity was too good to refuse, so, on 19 Jan 2023, I officially became the owner of Fernwood Loganholme.

Building a house and learning how to be a multi-site franchisee made 2023 an interesting year. More than ever, I value the teams in both clubs, led by my incredible club managers, Kate Thomas and Ash Martland. Superstars!

IT WAS ALL WORTH IT IN THE END

One of the interesting things about owning gyms is that you never know what the day will bring. I always have a plan for the day, but I accept that it must be fluid. For instance, I could be planning to do book work but end up fixing a toilet seat. I've learnt to be ready for anything.

During my 15 years of being a part of the Fernwood network, I've been so fortunate to have experienced many funny, sad, beautiful, and inspirational stories, all of which stem from the wonderful community of women who trust us to support them on their health and fitness journeys. Seeing the friendships that form between our members through attending the same reformer Pilates class, sweating their way through a FIIT30 session, or even having a coffee together after yoga is truly the best thing about running a Fernwood club.

I believe what goes around comes around. Our actions and choices have consequences. The choices we make about our own lives, the way we treat others, our contribution to society

– it's all a matter of cause and effect. Making thoughtful choices now ensures a favourable future. It's a belief that has served me well so far in business and in life.

Kim
RIMMER

WHEN LIFE TAKES AN UNEXPECTED TURN

My husband Clint and I ran a successful electrical business for over two decades before life took an unexpected turn. While driving to a job site, Clint's vehicle was hit head-on by a drug driver on a notorious stretch of road. It could have been a double fatality, but, fortunately for us, Clint survived and began the long rehabilitation process, going from wheelchair to recovery over the course of several years.

Due to his injuries, Clint could no longer work as an electrician, so we needed to find a new path for our family. After working together for so many years in our electrical business, we decided running another business together was the thing to do. Once you've been a business owner, going back to working for someone else can be difficult. I knew building a successful business was hard work. I had seen it with our electrical business, and I had seen it with my father's engineering business, so I knew what I was in for. Luckily, hard work was instilled in me from a young age. Given our options, I was determined to start a new business and put everything into making it a success. The next step was to determine what that business would be.

FINDING A NEW PATH

As a member of Fernwood Shellharbour, I loved seeing the owners, Adriana and Grace, in the club, and I loved seeing the joy they got from their jobs, supporting women in their health and fitness journeys.

When we saw Fernwood Woonona come up for sale, I thought, *How hard could it be to run a gym?* Boy, was I in for a shock, especially in the first few long years, with all the 1000-hour weeks. I didn't know what I was getting myself into.

In April 2014, Clint and I travelled to Melbourne to meet Di and present our business plan to her and a small panel. I cringe now at how inexperienced and fresh we were with our ideas, knowledge of the industry, and overall plans. However, Di obviously believed in us because our application was approved, marking the beginning of our Fernwood journey. Little did we know, it would take several years and many lessons before we really understood the fundamentals of running a successful club. In fact, the learning never stops.

HOW HARD COULD IT BE?

Without fitness industry experience, the early days of running the club posed a real challenge, so hiring the right people to support me was extremely important. Over time, I built a team of women who understood my vision and could challenge my ideas while putting forward their own.

It soon became apparent that my primary role within the club would be sales and marketing, an area I hadn't known I had a talent for but one in which I soon excelled. I was constantly thinking of ways to build our membership base, and I loved the challenge of growing the business. I'm very competitive, which means I set the bar high, and I'm continually seeking improvement and self-development. In business and in life, my competitiveness has been an asset.

Over the course of a few years, we grew our member base from 600 to 1600 members, which came with its own set of challenges. Our club is in a large heritage picture theatre, and the town planning from a century prior didn't take into account the possibility of 1600 women joining a gym. Parking became a major issue. However, the COVID pandemic temporarily solved that problem, knocking our membership numbers down until we were able to rebuild.

SOME SAY I'M IMPULSIVE

The best thing about running a Fernwood club is the flexibility to be your own boss, make your own rules, and create financial freedom. Over the past few years, I've been able to do things for myself and my family I would never have thought possible. I also love being able to provide jobs for so many wonderful women on my team. Quite a few are building careers with Fernwood, and I love seeing them grow in their roles. My team knows that when I run into the building, coffee in hand, and say, "Picture this…" they're about to get hit with yet another ambitious idea, project, or event.

When I won franchisee of the year in 2022, Di asked me, "Kim, would you say you're impulsive?" The answer? Yes, I would say I'm impulsive. I come up with an idea and execute it quickly. One fault of this approach is I often work faster than my team, but my impulsiveness and determination have undoubtedly contributed to my success. If I didn't take chances, I wouldn't be where I am today.

In business, staying ahead of the trends is vital. I'm always looking for what's coming and what women want. If you don't stay ahead of the market, you'll fall behind. For example, I was the first Fernwood club to open a recovery studio because I saw how important recovery was for overall health and fitness. Essentially, I recognised it as an important part of the fitness industry's future.

Another perk of being a Fernwood club owner is that I've had the rewarding opportunity to create a tribe of women who come together to not only support their health and fitness goals but also each other. Whenever there's a member in need, we all rally around them, whether they need fund-raising or moral support. When one young mum lost her husband to brain cancer, we held a fundraiser, and the out-pouring of support from our tribe and the local community was amazing. It has truly been a blessing to watch our in-club community blossom and grow.

IT'S A LITTLE EMBARRASSING BUT...

You might assume that buying a Fernwood club meant I got into the best shape of my life. Unfortunately, that wasn't the case. I actually put on 20 kg when I took over the club – but it gets worse. I'd often bump into friends and acquaintances at the shopping centre, and they would look at me, confused, saying, "Didn't you buy a gym?" Yep, that really happened.

After experiencing lockdowns and menopause, I learnt to put myself first and prioritise my health and fitness. It's not about the number on the scale but about how you feel, and now I feel strong and confident. I love my weekly fitness routine.

Exercising outside of my business has been beneficial, as I learnt to separate the businesswoman from the woman on a health and fitness journey. I'm still a member of Fernwood Shellharbour, and I'm grateful to have been welcomed into their beautiful tribe.

NEVER TAKE LIFE FOR GRANTED

I have four grown children, two of which, my two daughters, support me as club managers. I can say without bias that my girls are two of the hardest-working people on my team.

Working with family can definitely be a challenge, especially when it comes to maintaining a good work-life balance. Setting boundaries and work hours is extremely important to us. We have rules around when we can and can't discuss work, and we ensure that we communicate effectively in the club so we don't have to discuss work at home. With a mum who constantly wants to say, "Picture this…" it can be a challenge.

Without a doubt, Clint's accident reshaped our lives, forcing us onto an unexpected path. It also taught us not to take life for granted, and it's a lesson we live daily.

Caitlin **JURY**

A PASSION IGNITED

When I bought my first Fernwood Fitness club, I was quite young. My husband and I didn't have a lot of money, so I bought a struggling club for a lower financial investment. We struggled in the early years, doing everything possible to pay the staff and keep the lights on, even if it meant moving into my mum's garage.

Before buying my own club, I worked in the Mitcham club in multiple roles: group fitness instructor, personal trainer, sales, and club management. It was here where I first met Di. She came into the club for a speaking event when I was a club manager. The club owners were running late, and it was a busy day. I was worried we wouldn't be able to give Di the best greeting when she arrived. However, when she strolled into the club, she immediately took off her blazer, rolled up her sleeves, and helped me put out the chairs for our members before she spoke. It was inspiring to see someone who I idolised not hesitate to jump in and do what needed to be done. Di always put the members first, and it's a mindset I carry to this day.

It was my time working in the club that ignited my passion for the franchise and the Mitcham club in particular. I knew I wanted to do it all myself, so, in 2009, I made some big sacrifices, bought the Clayton club, and aimed to turn it around, which would be a monumental task. However, I knew what a successful club looked like, so I never doubted that we would get there in the end.

In 2014, the birth of my twin girls was a pivotal moment in my life and my business. I now had an even stronger motivation to change the trajectory of the club and ensure that it thrived so we could thrive too.

Thankfully, I was right to trust in my abilities, as we managed to triple the club's membership base, completely turn it around, and sell it in top condition in 2019. With that big goal completed, I needed a new challenge.

CHASING A DREAM

After selling the club, I planned to step away and try something new. I was doing some consulting, training other clubs, but I was always looking for something more.

At the beginning of 2020, Di asked me to take on a role at head office. I thought it would only be short-term; however, it led to me becoming general manager and working alongside Di for almost three years. It was a fantastic experience, and I learnt a lot. However, my passion was still with the clubs, particularly the Mitcham club. Ever since the club became company-owned in 2016, I had been asking to buy it, but I was always turned down. Regardless, I never gave up hope or stopped asking, even at the expense of sounding like a broken record.

Finally, in late 2022, my dream came true, and I became the proud owner of Fernwood Fitness in Mitcham.

A MINDSET FORGED FROM STRUGGLE

The earlier struggles at my first club taught me the value of resilience, maintaining a positive mindset, and always taking another step forward, no matter how hard it feels.

On my Fernwood journey, I had some good mentors, many of them other franchisees, who guided me along the way. In particular, Donna Hudec, Fernwood's current CFO, was a great source of wisdom, especially when I was in the general manager role. She taught me a lot about managing cash flow and forward planning, which has influenced the way I manage my second club. In business, cash flow must be your number one priority. There will always be problems that need fixing, for example, broken equipment, faulty electronics, a leaky roof, but if you don't focus on sales and revenue, you'll struggle to stay on top of the maintenance.

But that doesn't mean money should be your only focus. Another key to running a successful business is to stay positive and look after the people around you. Positivity spreads, so keep it up in yourself, and your staff will stay positive too, as will your customers, creating an amazing environment that everyone wants to be a part of.

As well as looking after your staff and customers, you must look after yourself too. Sometimes, as bosses, we tend to look after our staff first – I know I often did. However, my kids taught me that I am a better mum, wife, boss, and businessperson when I look after myself too.

With that in mind, I always put my family first so I don't miss any of the good stuff. I'm fortunate to love my job, so having a work-life balance is relatively easy. I love the club environment, and I love being there, even if it's just to exercise, clean, or chat to members and staff. Seeing the success of our members fills me with joy. I love seeing how we turn ladies in baggy clothes, barely looking at us when they first walk in, into thriving, confident women in brightly coloured leggings. Before they know it, they're joining our challenges, making friends with other members, and kicking fitness goals. It's an awesome reality we get to witness every day.

The good part about owning a gym is I get to train right alongside our members. I love weight training, and I still teach group fitness classes. Personally, I like to exercise five days a week. I know the health benefits of regular exercise; I explain them to our members all the time, so I can't let them or myself down by not prioritising my own training. Even when I'm super busy, I still find time to train.

I live by the motto "just do something." Perfectionism kills progress. The key is to do something, *anything*, with whatever tools you have access to right now. We should always aim to be moving forward.

Jessie ANDERSON

AN INDEPENDENT THINKER

My journey as a Fernwood club owner has been one of self-discovery, growth, and opportunities.

I joined Fernwood as a 17-year-old girl, finding my passion for fitness and health after I had my first child. Like many first-time mothers, I struggled with my weight as I tried to re-establish my relationship with food while combating post-natal depression. When my trainer threw me a lifeline and helped me find myself again, it was a pivotal moment in my life, igniting my love for exercise and a holistic lifestyle.

Fast-forward 12 years, and I not only maintained my health but also quit my profession as an accountant to become a personal trainer with no other fitness franchise than Fernwood!

In 2015, when an opportunity arose to own the club where I worked, it was a no-brainer. It felt like everything I had done up until that moment had been in preparation for this journey, and I was more than ready to start running my own club so I could help other women like me – help guide them, nurture them, and provide them with a safe and supportive environment in which they could thrive.

HOW I'M STILL STANDING

As a club owner, I've learnt that customer service is the key to success. It's at the core of everything we do. When we compromise our customer service standards, we risk our reputations, any goodwill we've earned, and ultimately our bottom line.

Our members trust us with their wellness and fitness journeys; hence, it is our greatest responsibility and promise to serve them and guide them to the best of our abilities. In life, nothing is perfect, and, every now and then, we can fall short on that promise. However, having a clear understanding of what 'customer service' means to us helps us rectify situations with ease and without prejudice.

As someone with ADHD, I've learnt to be extremely organised, and I have a rule to always handle the most difficult tasks first thing in the morning when I have the most clarity of mind. I also have a daily journal and calendar that I follow strictly. I make it a point to always complete the task at hand instead of giving into the everyday madness of running a business, which sometimes means saying 'no' to certain things. It's very important for me to be able to compartmentalise tasks so I don't lose focus on what's relevant now. It's vital that I always focus on tasks that are *important*, not just those that are *urgent*.

All business owners face ups, downs, and everything in between. In my case, I've learnt to look beyond the daily challenges and concentrate on the solutions rather than the issues themselves.

One big challenge was the COVID lockdown in March 2020. It was a new situation to every business owner, one that no amount of training would have prepared us for. During the pandemic, I learnt resilience and how to be nimble in my thinking. Almost every fortnight, we had to make business decisions to be compliant with the government mandates.

During this difficult period, I also learnt to be flexible. While it's imperative to always have a plan in place for every aspect of the business, sometimes things don't go according to plan, as was the case when the pandemic hit. To survive in a competitive industry, even in the good times, we must be flexible. When I plan, I have a backup and a backup to that backup. The key is to stay focused on the outcome, even if the path to get there changes. It's the destination I'm interested in and if I need to change my route or vehicle along the way, then so be it.

During lockdown, with the help of the wonderful NSO (head office) staff, we quickly adapted to virtually streaming classes. With changing mandates, we eventually introduced outdoor boot camps. We didn't know what life after the first lockdown would look like, and preparing the club to reopen was an enormous task.

Throughout all of it, it was crucial for me to remember that I was a leader to my team and they looked to me to reassure them that they would have a job to come back to when it was over. It was a tough time, but I learnt true grit and discovered that I'm capable of weathering any storm. No matter how strong it is, once it's over, I'll still be standing.

EVERY DAY IS A PRIVILEGE

The best aspect of running a Fernwood club is the fact that I get to make a positive impact in the lives of others. I've worked with some wonderful women over the years, and I take immense pride in knowing that I had a small part to play in helping them become who they are today. It is a privilege to be able to do what I get to do every day.

I've seen so many women walk through the doors on their first day, unsure, timid, perhaps a little intimidated. Before long, they're vibrant, confident, with smiles that reach their eyes. I smile too, knowing they trusted me on that first day and took a leap of faith!

While our members are truly inspirational, I've also had the privilege to have some amazing women on my team. One of the most satisfying aspects of the job is helping, empowering, teaching, guiding my staff to be amazing at their jobs and in life! It fills my heart to watch my younger team members blossom. I keep in touch with a lot of them, and I like to think I had a little part to play in preparing them for work and life in general.

A WORK IN PROGRESS

In life, we come across all kinds of people. Some will love you; some will tolerate you, and some will despise you. There's no control over how other people perceive you or what they say about you. I believe life is too short for me to live in fear of upsetting people. I can't please every single person who orbits my world. To live a life true to myself, all I need to do is the right thing, for me, for others, to the best of my ability. My best is all I can do.

My upbringing, family values, past wins and losses have all shaped me into the person I am today. I've always been an independent thinker, with a slight dose of stubbornness. My parents taught me the value of hard work from a very early age. My mum is all about people, always leading by example, wholeheartedly giving to those in need. She taught me to respect others the way I would like to be respected. My dad taught me to be a hard worker and to take risks, explore, and always do what makes me happy. My losses in life have taught me to be humble. Success, like everything else, won't last forever, so it's important to make the most of it while you've got it. While I'm thankful for the person I am today, I'm still a work in progress, and I'm excited to discover my future self.

I'VE LEARNT THROUGHOUT MY JOURNEY THAT *dwelling on things* I CAN'T CHANGE DOES NOTHING BUT NEGATIVELY AFFECT *the present moment.*

Larni MAILER

— NORTH LAKES, QUEENSLAND —

COMMUNITY IS EVERYTHING

Before the COVID pandemic, I was a stay-at-home mum, with a 1-year-old daughter and 16-year-old son. When we moved from Noosa to Brisbane, I didn't know anyone in the area, and my husband was FIFO (fly-in fly-out), so I joined the Fernytribe, not only for my health and fitness but also for the community.

Going to the club quickly became the highlight of my day. My daughter loved the creche, socialising with all the other children and playing with all the different toys. For both of us, it was the daily outing we needed.

During the COVID pandemic, lockdowns forced the club to close, and, as I lived close to the club and had business management experience, I offered my assistance to the club owner. I helped out where I could, and, when the club reopened, I was offered the club manager position. I was currently going through IVF (in-vitro fertilisation), trying for another child, and I still had my daughter to care for. However, the club owner fully supported me on my IVF journey and allowed me to work around my daughter and her needs. I was extremely lucky to work with a woman who was so understanding and supportive.

In 2020, my husband and I had a successful IVF transfer – we were over the moon! I was incredibly sick during the first months of the pregnancy, and I received so much care, compassion, and support at Fernwood, which helped a lot.

At 17 weeks, our pregnancy was labelled 'high-risk', and we were advised that, when I went into labour, a hysterectomy would be required due to where the baby was attached. To say we were scared is an understatement.

AN INDESCRIBABLE HEARTBREAK

We began the interview process to find my replacement, and, the entire time, my employer was supportive, caring, and continued to make me feel crucial to the business and the handover.

Twenty weeks into the pregnancy, I was admitted to hospital to await the arrival of our baby girl. During this time, the club owner, the team, and even our tribe of members continued to support me. Their phone calls, visits, and messages helped uplift me over a very long four weeks that overlapped with Christmas and the new year, a time I was forced to spend in hospital away from my family.

At 24 weeks and three days, my body couldn't hold out any longer, and I was taken to surgery for the far-too-early delivery of our baby girl, Arlo. She was so, so small and utterly perfect, and we weren't given enough time with her. She passed away in my arms 23 hours and 23 minutes after she was born.

There are no words for the heartbreak of being in a maternity ward with a butterfly on your door so others know you're saying goodbye to your child, whom you won't get to take home. The physical pain I was in meant a long recovery, and the emotional pain was unbearable.

Arlo's funeral was both beautiful and unbelievably cruel. Nobody should have to see a coffin that small and witness the pain of those trying to say goodbye. Sometimes, life can be far too hard.

My employer at Fernwood was at the funeral, as were my workmates and a sea of other faces, showing their respect and care for my family. Over the coming months, life around me went on while I tried to figure out what to do next. I was suffering from severe post-traumatic stress, and I didn't know how I was going to step forward. Although I had a fantastic psychologist and brilliant medical team supporting both my mental and physical recovery, I felt lost within myself.

WHEN A TRIBE COMES TOGETHER

During this time, my previous employer at Fernwood called to distract me with talk about the club. She even offered me my old role, saying I could return on my terms, ease back into it, take it a day at a time. I hesitantly accepted her offer.

The day I walked back into Fernwood, my heart was in my throat. I kept my head down and spent the day hiding in my office while one staff member after another visited me, often crying, to express not only their condolences but also their joy at having me back in the club.

A couple of weeks passed before I was able to make eye contact with our members. They knew I was in the club, struggling, trying to find my way back, and they gave me time and space. The level of respect shown to me during this time was critical in my journey to rebuild myself as a mum, a wife, and a woman. Slowly but surely, I stepped forward. I left my office, rejoined the members on the gym floor, rejoined my team – I stopped hiding. Then I started listening. Members approached me to share not just their condolences but also their own heart-aches, their own journeys of loss.

Not for the first time, this incredible tribe of women made me feel accepted, welcomed, and cared for. I wasn't alone in my journey, and I knew I never would be again. No matter what life threw at me, no matter what challenges and triumphs lay ahead, I knew that, in our tribe of women, we truly would empower each other.

A SURPRISE OPPORTUNITY

I managed that Fernwood branch for over four years before my family and I decided to move back north to the Sunshine Coast. Before the move, I resigned from my position to focus on some home renovations.

Five days after finishing at the club, I got a call from head office with a request for a meeting with Di regarding Fernwood North Lakes and an opportunity for me to become a franchisee. To say I was shocked would be an understate-ment. Not only did we live over an hour from North Lakes, but our daughter was about to start prep; we were in the middle of renovating and selling our house, and we were moving to a place where we once again didn't know anyone. My instinctual response was a firm 'no' to the meeting, but my curiosity won, and I agreed to chat with Di about the opportunity. The day before the meeting, I drove up the coast to see the club for myself so I knew what I was getting myself into.

That meeting with Di via Zoom was the first time we met, and it's a moment that will forever make me smile. I listened as the team from head office discussed the details of North Lakes, and Di commented that I should take a drive up and have a look in person. When I told her I already had, she smiled knowingly. In that moment, I think we both knew that Fernwood North Lakes was my next step.

NOT JUST A GYM, BUT A COMMUNITY

To me, the community Fernwood offered was everything. It was the key to my, and many other women's, health and wellness and an important part of our lives. With this in mind, I walked in the door of Fernwood North Lakes with three main goals:

1. To ensure our members understand that without them, there's no team, no me, no club and that Fernwood North Lakes belongs to them. I want each member to feel at home in our space, comfortable to make suggestions about improvements, listened to, and to have their opinion valued. With this direction, every new upgrade or addition is just as exciting to our team and members as it is to me. Our journey and joy are shared.

2. For the team of staff to wake up excited to help improve the lives of women on the daily. To do this, I want them to find their individual niche within the business and feel confident in taking on new training and moving into new roles better suited to their personalities. I want them to know, no matter what's going on in their lives, my door is always open, and support is always at hand.

3. For our space to be full of fun, fitness, and friendship. Priding ourselves on being the experts in women's overall health and wellness, and not just a gym, we continue to offer opportunities of interaction, workshops, social events, and challenges. With so many women utilising the same space, there's a constant opportunity to meet a new face, find a new connection.

In June 2022, Fernwood North Lakes was a small club. It had 540 members and needed time, attention, and love. I was blessed to be incredibly welcomed to the tribe, with the team not only willing but excited to implement changes, welcome new faces, and work on growth. Sixteen months later, we hit 1200 members, an achievement to say the least and a reflection of the teamwork, passion, and support of our community.

I've learnt throughout my journey that dwelling on things I can't change does nothing but negatively affect the present moment. We aren't guaranteed tomorrow, but we do have right now – a true blessing. So, I choose to live each day to its fullest, making the most of every hour, every minute, every second. No time should ever go to waste.

Melissa MCGLINN

— PETRIE & CARINDALE, QUEENSLAND —

THE PATH OF AN INDEPENDENT WOMAN

My family will tell you I've always been 'independent'; however, it was never more evident than when I packed up my son, left my then-husband, a dangerous relationship, and the small town we lived in, and moved to Brisbane to pursue a career in fashion and, consequently, a better future for my son.

As a broke, single mum with no support network around me, my independence proved vital in keeping our heads above water. I became the organisation queen, and, from the age of 5, my little mate was my gym buddy. It was a time well before 24/7 gyms, so I would bundle him up in his PJs, drag him to the gym at 4:45 am, and put him in the corner with his teddy and pillow to go back to sleep while I worked out.

I didn't have anyone but myself to rely on, and I had no choice but to make it work. Being ultra-organised was a trait that would be invaluable in my later role as a business owner.

I had been a member of Fernwood Carindale for ten years when we moved to an area with no Fernwood. I joined a mixed-gender gym instead – and I hated it!

At the time, I was still working in the fashion industry. However, a year later, I decided to hang up my high heels and do something different. In my fashion career, I loved helping women feel better about themselves and feel confident in their own skins, and I knew I wanted to empower women on a deeper level. So, when my husband asked me what I wanted to do, my answer was, "The only thing I really want to do is buy a Fernwood." And so began the next chapter of my story.

WAS IT THE RIGHT DECISION?

As part of the process of purchasing our first club – we eventually bought a second – we flew to Melbourne to meet Di and hopefully be approved as franchisees. From day one, she has always been warm and approachable. To this day, she still works tirelessly in the business, and I'm so grateful to be a part of the special brand she has built.

When we bought our first club, I instantly knew that my decision to change career had been the right one. I loved sharing the highs and lows with our members – it's something so special. I always say we're very good with tears, babies, and puppies! It's the daily conversations that make the club so special. Some are funny; some are sad, and some are inspirational.

Speaking of funny, when we first bought our Carindale club, we put in some new massage chairs. One Sunday, my husband and I were in the club doing bits and pieces, and Julie, one of our middle-aged members, was trying the chairs for the first time. Afterwards, she came to us, gushing, thanking us so much for the new chairs. "They're better than sex!" she said. My poor husband didn't know where to look. Our beautiful Julie still loves to embarrass him whenever she can.

In both clubs, I have an open-door policy, and my office is accessible to both staff and members. I love that my members are comfortable just stopping by to say hi.

FINDING STRENGTH IN TOUGH TIMES

Since becoming a Fernwood franchisee, there have been so many ups and downs, but, honestly, the COVID pandemic really put us to the test. I'll never forget the emotions I felt when having to close the doors of our beautiful club to our members, who needed us so much. Then I had to tell my staff they didn't have a job and I didn't know how long for.

At the time, having to constantly be the strong one was overwhelming. I had to find a way to not only overcome the administrative challenges but also to find a way to continue to engage and support our members through such a tough time.

Honestly, the way our amazing bunch of franchisees supported one another was simply amazing, and I'll forever be thankful to Di for keeping us as positive and busy as possible, although I think we may all still be traumatised by webinar fatigue!

PAST INFLUENCES AND NEW ROUTINES

My days as a single mum continue to influence how I go about my daily and weekly routines. I still food prep on a Sunday for the week ahead, and I set weekly goals and priorities for myself and the businesses.

Every single day, I have a list of priorities – I love a list! I always work backwards in planning what I must get done in a day so I can allow time blocks for everything. That being said, being in the club can be demanding, and that open-door policy of mine means I often get sidetracked. The team knows that if my door is closed, I'm trying to get stuff done, and they give me space when needed.

I would like to say I get into the gym every day at 5 am and do a workout or class like I used to, but unfortunately that isn't the case. It is, however, a goal for this year. In the meantime, I try to do either a HYPOXI, reformer, or weights workout in the middle of the day when the clubs are quieter. Everyone thinks of me as an extrovert; however, I really am an introvert, and I need time on my own to just be in silence. When working out in the club, I often put in my earbuds, even if I don't turn them on. Most people understand that it's my time and I need it to recharge.

Outside of the club, I love walking in nature, either by the seaside or in the bush surrounding our home. It keeps me grounded, and it's good to have no one to answer to, if only for a while. The businesses can fill my head 24/7, and sometimes I just need to turn off, so, often while driving, I'll listen to true crime podcasts or throw on some old bangers like Abba or Dolly Parton to sing out loud to.

I also love jumping into FIIT30 classes when I get the chance, as they're short and sharp, and I love the fun and comradeship of the small groups. There's always so much laughing to accompany the pain!

WE HAVE A CHOICE

Everything in life is a learning – the good and the bad – and the challenging experiences help shape us into who we become.

If I hadn't experienced being a broke single mum, or lived through an abusive relationship, I wouldn't be the strong person I am today, with an ability to relate to and a desire to champion other women. If we don't learn from our mistakes, they remain mistakes when they could instead become powerful lessons.

ULTIMATELY, *our health,* **OUR FAMILIES, OUR TRUE FRIENDS, AND KINDNESS ARE THE** *most important* **THINGS IN LIFE.**

Vanessa
PAUL

— MAROOCHYDORE, QUEENSLAND —

GIVING BACK TO THE COMMUNITY
IN EVERY WAY POSSIBLE

As a registered nurse on the Gold Coast for 20 years, I really enjoyed helping others. In 2008, I recognised the opportunity to be part of another sector of the health industry and loved the idea of assisting women with preventative healthcare, which led to me purchasing Fernwood Fitness Maroochydore.

I first met Di at the annual Fernwood conference in the early days of owning my club when I was a finalist for franchisee of the year. Di greeted me warmly on stage and congratulated me for my achievement. In my experience, she has always been approachable and happy to help in any way she can. She's truly a great role model to us all.

In 2015, I moved from the Gold Coast to the Sunshine Coast to be more involved in the business, working in the club daily. Once I started in the club, I fell in love with the positive environment and the endless opportunities to encourage, inspire, and nurture women. Previously, working in healthcare, I had worked with oncology nurses who always went above and beyond to make their clients' days the best they could be, and I wanted to do the same for our members. Every day is a gift.

Eventually, I purchased a second club, expanding to the Gold Coast. I had lived on the Gold Coast for most of my life, and I always knew the potential of the Fernwood gym in Robina. At that point, I had been operating Fernwood Maroochydore for ten years, and the opportunity came at the right time. As a bonus, it allowed me to reconnect with friends and family on the Gold Coast.

ONE BIG FAMILY

Within our clubs, we all support one another. We're like a big family, and members often tell me that the club is their second home. It's so rewarding to see ladies coming to the gym, gaining fitness, strength, confidence, and changing their lives for the better. We're so proud of our team, which always goes above and beyond to assist our members, empowering them to shine.

The key is to treat others how you like to be treated. You'll be amazed at the generosity and kindness you receive in return! You should also look after your team members and let them know how much you appreciate them. When they feel happy and supported, it flows on to your members, creating a positive environment for all.

While running a business is a full-time commitment, I ensure I have flexibility for any of my two children's special events. I also make sure our family time is spent well together. We love to walk down to the beach with our puppies, shoot some hoops, or just relax together as much as possible.

Ultimately, our health, our families, our true friends, and kindness are the most important things in life. It's vital that we surround ourselves with people who fill our cups and bring us happiness, which is exactly what I've done.

MAKING A POSITIVE IMPACT

For several years, I dealt with an ongoing domestic violence situation, which made maintaining our beautiful clubs challenging. However, through the support of my amazing teams and the Fernwood National Support Office, we made it through.

My experience during this difficult time re-emphasised the importance of providing a female-only space, where women from all walks of life can feel safe and supported. Over the years, I've championed DV Safe Phone, an organisation that collects, repurposes, and gifts mobile phones to victims of domestic violence through registered charities, safe houses, and authorities serving this vulnerable community. We also support, and are really impressed by, the work that our Fernwood community has done with the RizeUp organisation, from collecting toys at Christmas to furnishing safe, new homes for victims of domestic violence.

I'm fortunate to have such a great team, and we really enjoy interacting with our members and supporting local charities and events. We strive to do as much good as we can for the community. Giving back is so important. You never know the impact that even a small act can have on someone's life.

Adriana & Grace
AMPUERO BENAVENTE

DREAM, BELIEVE, ACHIEVE

Adriana was already a Fernwood member when she attended a four-day motivational course in 2001 that focused on the power of the mind and positive thinking. A key theme of the course was making your passion a business to create balance in your life.

She resonated with the Fernwood vision – to empower women to shine – and loved how she felt when she was at the club. Essentially, she had found her passion. The next step was to convert it into a business by becoming a Fernwood franchisee.

If Adriana was going to run a club, she knew she needed help, someone she could trust completely. So, she asked her sister Grace to be her business partner, and they, along with their husbands, applied to become Fernwood Franchisees, proposing a site in Shellharbour.

FUELLED BY PASSION

In 2001, Di and John visited Shellharbour and saw potential in the area. Even better, they approved our proposal. *Yes!* We were jumping up and down with joy. When we met Di, we already knew her story and vision for Fernwood, and we were inspired by her mission. She's such a motivational and down-to-earth person with a beautiful heart and a caring, compassionate attitude. Her energy, inner strength, and vision to grow the company are all remarkable. She's an inspiration to so many women, and we were proud to become members of the Fernwood family.

In May 2002, Fernwood Shellharbour officially opened its doors, and we never looked back. We've now been in business for over two decades, with lots of challenges, successes, and great moments.

Over the years, we've seen and lived all the gradual changes in club operations, procedures, and appearance, from completing memberships manually to the sophisticated systems we now have in place, from advertising in newspapers and on TV to using social platforms, from fixed operating hours to 24/7 club access, from membership cards to 24/7 access keys, from green-blue to hot pink, from basic services to nutrition, personal training, FIIT30, reformer Pilates, Hypoxi – always something new! Oh boy, did we go through so many changes, constantly learning, adapting, and staying ahead of the competition. In business, continuing to evolve as new ideas and technologies come along is crucial. The businesses that go the distance are the ones that are adaptable and willing to make the necessary changes. Fortunately, Di understands this, and Fernwood is constantly evolving.

PUSHED TO OUR LIMITS

Being in business for so long has made us stronger, more adaptable to change, and more resilient in difficult situations. In 2008, the global financial crisis hit us hard. It was the scariest and most challenging time of our lives. We took some big losses and had to make many sacrifices to survive.

By then, we had already helped so many women, and we didn't want to give up on our business. We weren't just supporting our members but also employing some great, highly skilled women. Our club is more than just a gym; it's a strong community, where real friendships are formed. We educate and empower women to invest in themselves to become the best they can be, with strength of mind, body, and spirit. We give them the opportunity to try different things, get to know their bodies, challenge themselves, learn what they can achieve, all while improving their health and wellbeing. It's so rewarding when we hear that our members' health issues have improved or cleared up completely thanks to the services we provide, or that women battling mental health issues consider our club their heaven or refuge, or that busy mums appreciate having some quiet time to work on themselves, knowing that our creche staff will look after their children as if they're their own. Our club was, and still is, our passion. We were willing to do whatever it took to save it, and we fought every day to keep our doors open.

Honestly, during this time, we were tested to the maximum – it almost broke our fighting spirit. However, with patience, hard work, a great team, and a supportive head office network, we survived and gradually rebuilt to thrive again.

Then, of course, the COVID pandemic hit in 2020, and the challenges began all over again. This time, however, we were well-equipped with the skills and mindset needed to get through it. Through proactive thinking, we were able to keep the business alive while supporting our team and keeping our members motivated. With every challenge we overcome, we only get stronger.

SURVIVING THE CRAZY TIMES

When we first opened our club, we were both young mums with three small children each. To manage the workload, we joined forces with our husbands to share responsibilities and ensure that our kids didn't miss out on doing their own activities and we didn't miss any special moments. We were also blessed with a wonderful grandmother, who helped us in so many ways.

When taking on any big challenge, it's important to have a good support network. We couldn't have done it all alone, and we're grateful for all the help we've received over the years.

As club owners, we've also received a lot of guidance from others. When running a business, it's important to let go of your ego and be open to learning from the people around you, whether they're your team members, your business partner, or someone else offering good advice. Just because it's your business, it doesn't mean you have all the answers. We can't know it all, and it's important to watch, listen, and learn as much as possible along the way.

Communication, organisation, and putting procedures in place are also critical. Everyone in your business should know what you're trying to achieve, so you need clear targets and a good action plan.

As busy club owners, we've found that it's important to make time for things that energise us so we can project that energy to our team. Certain activities, such as reading a book, dancing in a Zumba class, or a good strength training session, leave us feeling refreshed and ready to face the challenges of the day. What we market to women is what we practise, and it's important that our members and team see us enjoying our club services as much as them. We love training in the club, seeing our own results, and living the Fernwood experience alongside our members.

Our kids are now all grown up, and we often question how we survived those crazy times when they were young. Looking at them and all they've achieved in life, we can see that we did a pretty good job, but we didn't do it alone. Never be too proud to ask for help, and always make sure you've got a good support network to back you up when times get tough. Life gets busy, and it's important to stop, enjoy the special moments, and make some good quality time for yourself.

A DREAM COME TRUE

We've certainly come a long way since we decided to turn our passion into a business. Since the beginning of our Fernwood journey, we've held the "dream, believe, achieve" mindset. *Dream* big or small – dreaming is the first step to achieving anything. *Believe* in your potential and act to realise your dream. Finally, *achieve* everything you set out to do.

If you surround yourself with like-minded people and put yourself in a positive environment, the journey to realising your dreams will be much smoother. Additionally, spiritual richness is a powerful tool that can help you contribute to the world and make a positive impact on the people around you. While everyone's journey is different, certain truths remain the same.

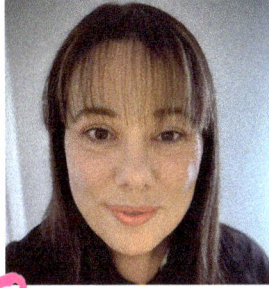

Emma
GADE

— ST AGNES, SOUTH AUSTRALIA —

EVERY CHALLENGE IS
AN OPPORTUNITY

Growing up with parents who were both blind, I didn't have a typical childhood. As you can imagine, a number of things were difficult for our family, but the challenges forced me to be more independent much earlier than most people.

From a very young age, I felt that I needed to – and could – look after myself. I've carried that same confidence into my adult life, and it has been pivotal. I know that, at the end of the day, even if things get tough, I have the strength to get through it. I've also come to understand the importance of driving myself in a positive direction to get the most out of life.

At age 21, when my first son was born, it changed my life. I was relatively young, and suddenly having someone dependent on me made me quickly realise where my priorities lay. While other friends were out partying, I focused on building a home and earning money to provide for my child.

LITTLE DID I KNOW, I WAS EMBARKING ON A MASSIVE JOURNEY

As a young mum, I was looking for a way to stay fit. One day, in 2002, when walking through a local mall, I noticed that a new gym was soon opening – the name of that gym was Fernwood Fitness. I loved the concept and immediately signed up as a member, officially beginning my Fernwood journey.

After attending the gym for a while and getting to know the staff, I asked if they had any work available. As it turned out, they did, and I started work on the front desk. Over time, I worked my way up through the ranks, eventually becoming club manager. Because it was a company-owned club, I worked directly for Di and her team. I quickly found her to be an amazing role model for all women, showing us what we can achieve through hard work. Even though she's a busy woman, she always takes the time for me and other franchisees when we need her. Di's vision has played a huge role in shaping the organisation into what it is today.

As a club manager, my passion for the brand was immense, and, in 2016, Fernwood offered me the opportunity to buy the club and become a franchisee. Of course, I accepted the offer, and I've been running the club ever since.

THERE IS A LESSON IN EVERYTHING

Due to my experience as a club manager, I was comfortable operating the gym when I became a club owner. However, I did face a big challenge when it came to the financial side of the business. Luckily, I had a great support network around me, and I'm very grateful.

As a club owner, you quickly realise that the saying "you can't please all of the people all of the time" is very true. I've come to realise that all I can do is my best and hope it's enough to please most people. Overall, the good times and good people far out-weigh the challenges, and I'm very blessed to have a job I enjoy.

In business, challenges will always arise, but I believe there's a lesson in every difficult situation. If you don't learn from going through a tough time, then you've gone through it for nothing. Never let a good challenge go to waste.

THE BATTLE TO MAINTAIN A GOOD WORK-LIFE BALANCE

Having a blended family of five children, life can get quite busy. My fiancé also has a demanding job, so we're frequently trying to maintain balance in our lives. In addition, my youngest son has autism and requires a significant amount of my time. The key for me is to make sure I'm always present in what I'm doing. If I'm with family, work isn't on my mind. If I'm at work, I work hard to try and get home as soon as possible.

As a business owner, finding a good work-life balance can be challenging. My business isn't just a job; its success ensures that our family is well looked after. Sometimes I'm torn between being with the family and working to provide for them. However, I do try to ensure we always have a family meal together at dinner time. It's a chance for us to all sit around and share the events of the day.

I've found that getting away from Adelaide as often as possible has really helped achieve a better work-life balance. Whether it's camping, glamping, going to the beach, or taking a driving holiday, these times present a real opportunity to disconnect from work and just enjoy the moment with family. A big thank you to my team members, who are so reliable and trustworthy, allowing me the opportunity to have these breaks.

As a business owner, surrounding yourself with positive, hard-working staff is so important. When you have a workplace where your team feels empowered and you trust them fully, everyone will be working at their best. I love my staff, and I'm dependent on them to help make my business a success. Without the great team I have around me, the club wouldn't be where it is today.

RESPONSIBLE ENERGY MANAGEMENT

I firmly believe that every day we only have so much energy to give, so we need to spend it wisely. I try to avoid getting too tied up with people and problems that are 'energy sappers'. I also make sure I put as much effort as possible into things that are ultimately going to be rewarding.

Every day, there's so much that competes for our time and effort, and we can easily get stuck committing far too much time to things that aren't important. In doing so, we can start to fall behind with important matters. Life is a balancing act and once we realise that some things are worth the effort and some aren't, we can put more energy into the tasks that are actually going to make a difference in our lives.

A DEEP WELL OF INSPIRATION

While I wouldn't be anywhere without my team, I feel the same about our members. Almost daily, a story of inspiration comes out of our club. Whether it's a woman returning to the gym after having a baby, a mother with grown-up kids deciding to get back into fitness, or any other one of the many reasons why our members are at the club, seeing women feeling empowered and confident is very inspirational.

Over the years, I've had a number of women call me directly and say, "I need help. I've lost my way and no longer really look after myself." They're usually women who have given it all to their family or a relationship and suddenly realise that their own health is suffering. Watching these women bravely fight back and reach and exceed their targets is the single most satisfying part of running a Fernwood club.

As a club owner, it's important to make your members feel invested. The truth is, there are many ways people can keep fit and healthy outside of a gym, so you must give them a reason to come and stay. I feel genuinely honoured each and every time a member signs up. I love watching their progression. The more a member feels that they're a meaningful part of the club, the more likely they are to stay and recommend the club to others. Therefore, it's imperative that you keep the 'member experience' in your thoughts with every decision you make.

WE ALL NEED
ACTIVITIES THAT
re-energise us
SO WE CAN
bring our best
TO THE
WORKPLACE.

Cathy
RUSSELL

THE PATH TO EMPOWERING WOMEN

My journey as a Fernwood club owner has certainly been unique. In 2005, my neighbour asked me if I was interested in becoming a Fernwood franchisee. She thought it would be perfect for me.

Her timing was excellent because, at the time, I had a prominent music studio in Sydney's Eastern Suburbs, and, with my own children in primary school, I was ready to start spending my workdays with adults. If I did decide to open a club, I could still run my music school with others teaching.

Music has always been a big part of my life. My dad teaching me to speed-read at age 8, combined with a photographic memory and a love of numbers, codes, systems, and language, made studying music a natural progression. My passion and dedication eventually led to me being recognised as the dux of the Sydney Conservatorium of Music.

To some, switching from teaching music to running a fitness club might have seemed like an odd move. However, to me, the opportunity seemed perfect. It was exactly what I was looking for.

A SERIES OF DEVASTATING EVENTS

In 2006, I opened a club in Rosebery, NSW, which we built from scratch. With the gentrification of the area, the club quickly grew, becoming a successful business.

My next club acquisition was Fernwood Fitness in Chatswood, which became the club with the highest percentage of personal training (PT) in the network, at approximately 38 percent PT at the time. Really, it was a boutique personal training club that suited the local demographic.

However, not long after starting the venture and splitting my time between Chatswood and Rosebery, the global financial crisis (GFC) hit, and it was tough, to say the least. Banks were upping interest rates for businesses with high risk factors, and, of course, gyms were a prime target. Luckily, my husband and I still had two other businesses, which saved us from meeting the same fate as many other gym owners.

In 2011, we downsized to one club, Rosebery, and, as the GFC receded, we focused on growth. Then, in April 2015, we made our next acquisition: Fernwood Fitness Rockdale. We had only owned Rockdale for a short time when the ANZAC Day hailstorm hit, decimating our Rosebery club. Roof, walls, equipment – all destroyed. Outside, there were piles of hailstones a metre high, looking like snow drifts in the streets. The scene was surreal.

Following the event, our members were at the forefront of my mind, and I marked out an area where we could continue limited operations during the eight months it took to rebuild the club. It was a soul-destroying experience, and I can't thank my beautiful club coordinator Sue enough for taking the brunt of the day-to-day operations while I worked at Rockdale, trying to expand from the 350 members we started with to the viable business it is today, along the way winning the St George Business Woman of the Year award, as well as multiple other awards for the business. Eventually, Rosebery was back in action – fully rebuilt and better than ever to be onsold to a new franchisee, allowing me to focus on Rockdale.

Like deja vu, in July 2022, when a severe storm hit our Rockdale club and blew out every window on the first floor, it looked like a bomb had hit it. Sue and I had flashbacks to the Anzac Day hailstorm; we couldn't believe we had been hit with yet another devastating natural disaster. Until repairs were completed, we had to close the club for business.

As you can see, my Fernwood journey has taken several unexpected twists and turns, but I've overcome every challenge along the way, which has helped me grow, both personally and professionally. I wouldn't be who I am today without those difficult moments.

A REAL INSPIRATION

The best thing about running a Fernwood club is that you get to help *all* women exercise and be healthy. At my Rosebery club, we had the *most* inspirational woman I've ever met. She was in a wheelchair and wanted to start exercising.

With the guidance of her trainer, she learnt to get in and out of her chair to move between weight machines. She also did Zumba and boxing in her chair and would crawl upstairs to participate in FIIT30.

She was an absolute legend and an inspiration to us all.

WORK HARD, PLAY HARD

When you work hard, it's important to make time for the little things that help you stay focused and motivated.

For an hour each day, I walk my two beautiful dogs while listening to the Spanish news and podcasts. I love to walk, walk, walk – it keeps me fit.

I also practise reformer Pilates, as it works every muscle group and, as an instructor, I can come up with new ideas for classes.

No matter how busy I get, I rarely let work get in the way of play. We all need activities that re-energise us so we can bring our best to the workplace.

THE DAY THAT DEFINED MY LIFE

Even after all the big challenges I've faced running my clubs, there's one day that defined the rest of my life.

One day, in March 2015, I collapsed at the Rosebery club. The last thing I remember is trying to get to the group fitness room, looking for help. The next thing I knew, I was waking up in the resuscitation unit at Prince of Wales Hospital. One month after taking over the Rockdale club and seeing my beautiful Rosebery club destroyed, I found out that I had bilateral breast cancer requiring a double mastectomy. I was devastated. Initially, I didn't tell anyone and kept trying to run my clubs while undergoing no fewer than seven operations. It was a tough time, to say the least, but the experience helped me better empathise with and empower women, a positive outcome of a difficult situation.

My diagnosis also led to the next pivotal moment in my life: walking El Camino in Spain with ten other women in 2017, raising $80,000 for breast cancer research. El Camino changed my life forever, and I've been studying and speaking Spanish ever since.

These days, I aim to take one holiday per month with my husband Garry. In 2024, I had already booked seven months' worth of holidays by March. It doesn't matter if they're overseas trips, road trips, or long weekends away, as long as I'm sticking to my one-per-month rule and checking in with the club daily. I should also mention that without my loyal, committed staff, it wouldn't be possible.

I now live life by the motto, "No viajo para escapar de la vida. Viajo así que la vida no me escapa," which translates to, "I don't travel to escape life. I travel so that life doesn't escape me."

BUILDING A TEAM *of great people* **WHO ALL SHARE THE SAME VISION IS CRUCIAL TO A** *business's success.*

Melissa & Paula
LEE LIM

NEVER SHY OF A CHALLENGE

In Asian culture, it's common for your mother-in-law to 'look down' on you if you're uneducated or don't have a good job. Knowing this, I (Melissa) grew up to be a fiercely independent woman. From an early age, my mother pushed me to aim high and strive for success, so I've never been shy of a challenge.

My business partner Paula and I met during Fernwood group fitness classes. On one Friday evening, during RPM class, we got talking about how 'cool' it would be to own a Fernwood club one day. A couple of years later, the opportunity arose, and we jumped on it.

EXPERIENCING THE
FERNWOOD DIFFERENCE

When my daughter Charlotte was 10 months old, I (Paula) returned to work. However, with all the challenges of being a first-time mum, I felt tired and unmotivated. Realising I needed to exercise, I joined a gym and signed up for boot camp. My fitness journey had officially begun.

Due to a minor injury, I took a break from strenuous exercise and got stuck into yoga. Once my injury improved, I realised I missed going to the gym and doing PT (personal training), so I googled local gyms and stumbled upon Fernwood Cannington.

As soon as I stepped into the club, I felt that the place was different. It had a real community vibe, and many of the members, trainers, and staff I met all became friends. One of them was Melissa Lee.

Mel and I did the same classes every week, which soon turned into every day. One day, we were both chatting about how amazing it was to have a 'business' that helped women be healthy and happy, a place where they looked after themselves with exercise and made friends. Two years later, I learnt that the owner of Fernwood Cannington was returning to England and looking to sell the club. We both agreed that we should seize the opportunity, so we began the application process, and, before long, we were the proud new owners of Fernwood Cannington.

A SERIES OF TOUGH LESSONS

We first met Di in person when we flew to Melbourne to discuss the possibility of taking over the Cannington club. She looked every part the confident CEO but with a level of authenticity and friendliness that were both unexpected and welcome. The meeting went well, and our application was approved.

Neither of us had a background in fitness or any experience running a business. As it turns out, it's a lot harder than it looks!

A big, unexpected challenge was finding good staff. In the beginning, we were too nice to let some team members go, even when they were detrimental to the business and harmony within the team. However, we soon learnt to be a bit more ruthless and prioritise harmony and positivity in the club over all else. Building a team of great people who all share the same vision is crucial to a business's success. We learnt this lesson, and several others, a little later than we would have liked, but better late than never.

ONE BIG HAPPY FAMILY

While we had no experience running a gym, we did receive some amazing support from other franchisees and the team at head office, which helped us navigate all the earlier challenges. Our staff have also been instrumental in our success, and we couldn't have done it without them. Investing in your employees is so important. If you look after and nurture them, the good ones will reward you with loyalty and excellent work. Keeping your staff motivated is a critical aspect of running a successful business.

We've worked hard to ensure our in-club community feels like a family. Members often cook meals or bake cookies and cakes to share with the staff. One member even painted some artwork for a team member's birthday, and we've been invited to several members' weddings, birthdays, and baby showers.

However, maintaining a close and vibrant community doesn't come without challenges. For example, when we first took over the club, I was surprised to learn how many women were struggling with life in general. Feeling like we needed to fix everything, we sometimes got involved in their personal lives. Essentially, we had to accept that we couldn't fix everything. We could, however, still listen and be there for our members when they needed us.

To many, Fernwood isn't just a 'women's gym'; it's so much more than that. Regularly, members tell us, "Fernwood is my happy place, my home, and my community." It truly is something special.

A POWERFUL AND POSITIVE ENVIRONMENT

For me (Melissa), the best thing about owning a Fernwood club is seeing how cheerful and inspiring our staff are. They're so happy to come to work, knowing they're empowering other women to shine.

We've created a really positive environment within the club. As a leader, staying positive, even in difficult times, is important, as positivity is infectious and rubs off on your staff and everyone else around you. Being empathetic towards your staff is also important. If you can show them that you genuinely care, they'll reward you with loyalty and respect. Most of our staff are mothers, and I love giving them the opportunity to help other women before going home to inspire their own kids.

WITH CHALLENGE COMES GROWTH

I (Paula) have one main goal in life: to always be kind, be helpful, be the one who makes people laugh, and be happy.

Life can be complicated and stressful, and taking things too seriously doesn't help the situation. In fact, it's no fun at all.

To maintain a healthy work-life balance, I've relied on the support of everyone around me – my husband Alvin, my daughter Charlotte, my parents, my staff. I can't imagine running a successful business while still having time for family without their understanding and support. Thankfully, I haven't had to do this alone.

When you're running a business, time really does become an issue, and I must constantly remind myself to make time for exercise. Some days, I'm forced to break my fitness routine to deal with challenges related to the club. However, when I do miss a class, members and instructors often approach me and say, "Where were you this morning? We missed you in class!" I'm fortunate to be surrounded by great people who keep me accountable.

Ultimately, becoming both a mum and business owner forced me to grow as a person. Every day is a new challenge, and I've learnt to think outside the box. For example, a marketing plan that worked last year won't necessarily work today. The industry changes so fast, so flexibility is key.

Since becoming Fernwood franchisees, we've been put to the test repeatedly, but, over time, we've built the wisdom, resilience, and adaptability to overcome anything that comes our way. We're always ready for the next challenge.

ULTIMATELY, FOLLOWING MY *own intuition* AND IGNORING THE *whispers of doubt* GOT ME WHERE I AM TODAY.

Sanela
MATANOVIC-LIKIC

A WOMAN WITH DREAMS

I once had a teacher who said that a man without dreams is a dead man. Oh boy, did I start to dream.

After surviving the horrible war in Bosnia, seeing my family lose everything and struggle to rebuild their lives, I was forced to leave the country. When I arrived in Australia with my husband as a refugee, I was only 21 years old. We left everything behind. We had no money, no family, and we didn't speak any English. However, I was determined to embrace my new life in Australia and make the most of every opportunity.

I started at Fernwood as a member, working on my own health and fitness journey. After the first COVID lockdown, I rejoined my local club with my daughter, as I wanted her to experience all the amazing things Fernwood had to offer, knowing she would be safe in a women-only gym.

One day, while working out in the club, I experienced a light-bulb moment. *Why not own a Fernwood club myself?* I thought. I mean, Fernwood had already made such a positive impact in my life, and I wanted to ensure that more women got to experience the same awesome community and comfort. To me, it wouldn't just be a business; it would be a passion.

STRENGTH IN THE FACE OF STRUGGLE

When I first heard that Di had won the Telstra Business Award in the 2000s, I never thought I would one day meet her. After approving me to become a franchisee, she said she believed in me and I would do well as a club owner. Her words took my confidence to the next level, and I'm so grateful for the opportunity to spread her vision.

Becoming a Fernwood Club owner was a rollercoaster ride filled with challenges, but every hurdle was worth overcoming in the end. The initial struggle kicked off with delays and setbacks due to the relentless nature of COVID-related disruptions and lockdowns. Navigating through an industry in which I had no prior experience added an extra layer of complexity, and the constant judgement from others fuelled my desire to do even better. Ultimately, following my own intuition and ignoring the whispers of doubt got me where I am today.

The turning point came with the club's grand opening. Everything seemed to fall into place, but the ease was short-lived, as the challenges evolved with the growing number of members and stresses related to running my own business. To tackle this, I made a conscious decision to surround myself with capable and competent people who shared my vision. Hiring a reliable team helped distribute responsibilities and manage the increasing demands. I'm still involved in all aspects of the business so I always know what's going on, but I now have a brilliant group of people supporting me.

Over time, I learnt that I need to forgive myself when I make mistakes and try to do better next time. I now know that every challenge is a stepping stone towards a greater purpose, and every setback is an opportunity for learning and growth.

My grandparents taught me the value of resilience and perseverance, which has helped me get through the tough times. I'm grateful for the strength they instilled in me. However, my late mother played the biggest role in shaping who I am today. I wish I could share this journey with her. I miss her every day.

MAINTAINING PRODUCTIVITY AND FOCUS

Establishing our club from scratch and continuing to nurture it has left little room for a work-life balance. However, as time goes on, I can imagine a point where that slowly changes and I can give myself permission to take time off and spend more time with family.

Because I'm so busy, my daily routine as a hands-on club owner is crucial to maintaining productivity and focus. I take immense pride in the gym's presentation and cleanliness, considering it a reflection of the positive environment we strive to create. Greeting members as they walk through the doors and seeing familiar faces has become a cherished routine. Engaging in meaningful conversations and connections with our members not only fosters a sense of community but also provides insights into their fitness journeys.

Being a gym owner doesn't make me immune to the same health and fitness challenges many of our members face. While I try to inspire and motivate others, often I need the same level of encouragement. However, seeing the effort our members put in and the changes that follow inspires me to keep pushing to do better every day.

FAMILY MAKES IT SPECIAL

For me, running a Fernwood club has become a source of immense joy, especially because I'm getting such amazing feedback from our members.

I also get to share countless moments with my daughter when we're working together. The collaborative effort between us not only strengthens our bond but also adds a personal touch to the club's atmosphere.

Equally special is the pride I feel knowing that my family overseas shares in our achievements. Their support from afar adds an extra layer of significance to the venture, making running our Fernwood club an incredibly fulfilling experience that extends beyond the club itself. Having a strong, supportive family has helped me navigate the challenging moments. Big credit goes to my beautiful daughter Uma – I couldn't do it without her.

Lee SQUIRE

— BALLARAT, VICTORIA —

A JOURNEY OF CHALLENGES AND TRIUMPHS

My love for movement began at age 3 and continued all throughout my life. At the early age of 13, I became a coach at the Sovereign Calisthenic College and ended up devoting over 25 years to calisthenics. In my teens, I expanded my passion to include ballet, gymnastics, and performing with local theatre companies and on TV.

Driven by my love for dance, in 1981, I began instructing fitness classes at a gym called Vigor, followed by 18 years at the YMCA. During those 18 years, I commuted to and from my corporate job in Melbourne while moonlighting as a fitness instructor, teaching classes in the evenings. In May 2000, I finally found my home, joining the Fernwood family as a group fitness instructor.

With extensive fitness industry experience and 18 years in the corporate world, purchasing Fernwood Ballarat felt like a natural progression. So, in October 2003, my husband Brian and I became the proud owners of Fernwood Ballarat.

THE REAL TEST BEGINS

I thought my previous experience would have prepared me for business ownership, but I was naive in that regard. At the time, Brian and I were raising three young boys – Ben, Jack, and Henry – so we felt the additional pressure.

Owning your own business is next level. The buck stops with you – full stop! Business is demanding and forever changing; it's not for everyone. It will teach you a lot about yourself and then some.

In the early days, mother's guilt stole a lot of my joy. I felt torn between my children and my business. I wanted the club to be a success, but I also wanted to be there for my kids. Whenever I had to leave them, I felt guilty, which led to further feelings of frustration, overwhelm, and anxiety. During this time, I made many poor, unhealthy choices, leading to alcoholism and some seriously tough times for myself and my family. I admitted myself to rehab for a life-changing 30-day experience, and I've now learnt to better manage my emotions, my reactions, my time, and I've made peace with my past. I have proudly been living a life of sustained sobriety since 2012, with a personal book release due in 2025. Being open about my struggles has helped others facing similar challenges.

Part of the problem was that I was a people pleaser, saying 'yes' to everyone but myself. In trying to please everyone and make their lives easier, I was the one who suffered. Eventually,

I learnt the power of saying 'no', and my life has improved considerably. 'No' can be a complete sentence – sometimes it's all you need to say. I now say no when I feel that it's necessary, and I accept that what others think is none of my business. You can't please everyone, and not everyone will like or support you, which is okay. That's life. You can't control what other people think or feel. So, remember to be you, stay true to yourself, be original. Learning to say no may seem difficult at first, but I assure you it makes life a whole lot easier in the long run.

Through the tough times, I remained inspired and driven by my vision of the possibilities and potential of Fernwood Ballarat. My passion for the business was like a flame I fanned, refusing to burn out no matter how challenging the situation grew. Over time, my resilience, resourcefulness, and commitment to succeed taught me to believe in myself fully, and I value the importance of taking consistent steps every day to bring me closer to my goals.

Now, whenever the negative thoughts start raging inside my head, I remind myself that anything worthwhile comes with unique challenges, and I must be present in the moment, for this too shall pass...

Due to the adversity I've experienced in life, I now have the courage, conviction, fortitude, patience, and strength to face the future with confidence. With each new challenge, I only grow stronger and wiser.

WHAT'S BEST FOR YOUR BODY IS BEST FOR YOU

For our bodies and minds to be at their best, we must give them what they need, which includes fresh air, sunlight, deep breathing, hydration, stress management, clean eating, movement, and sleep. By giving our bodies what they need, we improve our overall mood, along with our mental, emotional, and physical wellbeing, all while optimising our energy stores.

When life gets busy, having a clear daily routine can help us stay on top of our physical and mental health. Here's what a typical day looks like for me:

MORNING

- Lemon water. Staying hydrated because the human body is 60–70 percent water. Clean water keeps us clear and alert, flushing out toxins and eliminating waste.
- Gratitude journal.
- To gain clarity each morning, I ask myself five important questions:
    » What am I grateful for today?
    » What am I excited about today?
    » What am I committed to today?
    » What will make a difference today?
    » What would I do if I were not afraid?
- Fifteen minutes of sunlight for vitamin D combined with breathwork and gratitude.
- I love variety, so I mix up the following modalities morning and evening: rebounding, vibration plate, weights, Swiss ball, Pilates, stretching, and (my favourite) my inversion table.
- Daily cold shower for at least 2 minutes to boost my energy and immunity.
- I have naturally always intermittently fasted until 11 am.

- Cayenne pepper, lemon, and honey each day to boost health.
- Green juice daily.

EVENING

- Cycling or walking to unwind in nature and balance my brain, combined with focused deep-breath rituals to create homeostasis within my body.
- Teaching classes at the club – helping our members fills me with joy!
- Solitude for my soul and to reduce stress.
- Massage for emotional release.
- I've always been vegetarian by choice, so, naturally, I focus on consuming wholefoods with fewer chemicals. Making sound nutritional choices is important for maintaining health.
- Gratitude journal.
- Getting a good night's sleep – sleep is the key to longevity, health, and happiness. Melatonin, the sleep hormone, boosts the immune system and is a powerful antioxidant.

I also believe in celebrating and giving ourselves rewards, such as a massage or going to the beach to reset and rejuvenate. Rewarding ourselves not only boosts our mental health, but it also gives us something to look forward to when we've been working hard.

Essentially, I'm putting myself in a positive and productive mindset as early as possible, setting myself up for success all throughout the day.

IT TAKES A VILLAGE

When I purchased my club in 2003, I had no idea what the future had in store. I could never have predicted the challenges that lay ahead, nor could I have imagined the triumphs. There are so many moments, so many lessons, so many memories I'll always hold on to. They've shaped me into who I am today.

The old adage is true – it really does take a village. I feel thankful and honoured to have the support of Brian, my handsome partner in life. Together, we link arms with Jacqui, our club manager, and our passionate, professional team, which serves our members and helps our community manage their mental, emotional, and physical wellbeing.

We're also blessed to be surrounded by our incredible, supportive team at the national support office. Collaborating with the support office and other Fernwood franchisees has been an enriching experience. Everyone brings their unique talents and strengths to the table, all for the greater good. We share our challenges, our triumphs, and our learnings, asking one another for help when we need it. My network is my safety net – it's essential to my success. Whenever a new challenge arises, someone in my network always has the solution. I certainly wouldn't want to walk this journey alone! Thank you, everyone. Together, we make a difference, and I deeply appreciate and love the people in my village. Dream big!

I'm so proud to be part of the Fernwood empire, and I want to thank our founders for creating a sanctuary for women. Fernwood has been synonymous with Australian women's health and fitness for over three decades, and I don't see that changing anytime soon. Stronger together!

Kim
BULLOCK

— MORDIALLOC, VICTORIA —

A FUSION OF PASSION AND TENACITY

Before the COVID pandemic, I worked with big gyms. In my previous job, I had a wonderful boss who believed in me and helped me become a strong, independent leader. She took the time to develop my managerial skills, enough so that when she was finally promoted, I received her old job. Suddenly, I was in charge of 70 studios across Australia, Vietnam, and Thailand.

After 11 years in the fitness industry, the pandemic struck, and I was made redundant. For six months, I searched for work, but pickings were slim. There were plenty of people in the same position as me.

My redundancy and struggle to find work forced me to consider what I really wanted to do for the rest of my career. I decided that I wanted to work for myself so I was in charge of my own destiny, and I definitely wanted to be in the health, wellness, and fitness industry.

A friend and I had been discussing the possibility of opening our own gym. At the time, she was working at Fernwood. One day, in June 2021, she presented me with a concept Di Williams had been working on: Fernwood Fusion, a boutique wellbeing experience that included Pilates, barre, and yoga. The project required someone with experience running a business, knowledge of the fitness industry, and the ability to make changes on the fly. For me, it was the perfect fit.

Using the leftover money from my redundancy, I bought into the franchise, and, in 2022, we opened Fernwood Fusion Mordialloc.

BIG RISKS IN UNCERTAIN TIMES

Because Fernwood Fusion was an untested concept, we faced new surprises every day. Whenever an unexpected challenge presented itself, we had to think on our feet to find a solution. We had so many unanswered questions. Will the concept be popular enough to sustain our studio? Will the pandemic ever end? Will people return to group classes? There was so much uncertainty around the project. While Fernwood was already a successful brand, the Fusion concept was fresh, and we didn't know how it would land. Even so, I was confident in my abilities to drive the business, and I had faith in Fernwood's brand power to help push us through.

From day one, we worked tirelessly to make the project a success. While walls were being demolished and bathrooms were being built, we were out pounding the pavement, doing letterbox drops and pop-up stands in the cold Melbourne weather. Honestly, it was hard work and not my favourite part of the project.

Thankfully, the work paid off, and we opened our Mordialloc branch with enough members to pay the bills and provide me a wage. The project was a success.

UPLIFTED AND INSPIRED

As a Fernwood club owner, I'm very driven to provide a quality offering with the best instructors and outstanding customer service. My hand-picked staff are aligned with my goals, and our members feel the love. As I'm onsite most days, members know they can come to me directly with any feedback or just for a chat. When members tell me we've helped change their lives in a positive way, it's so uplifting. I have so many lovely stories, but one in particular stands out.

In 2023, a lovely lady came to the club and bought ten sessions. She disclosed that she had cancer and her doctor had approved exercise, but she didn't want to join as a member, as she didn't know how much time she had left. Hearing her story, we all felt quite sad.

Over the course of a year, she kept purchasing session packs, and we continued to work with her. We could see the positive impact the regular exercise was having on her wellbeing. Her appearance changed – she looked radiant – and her movements were constantly improving.

Recently, she came into the studio – looking like a million bucks, mind you – and, jumping up and down, she explained that her tumours were shrinking. Yes! Her doctor believed the exercise was helping and encouraged her to keep at it. She was so delighted with her progress that she joined as a member – no more short-term packs! We all cried happy tears at the news.

THE EVOLUTION OF LIFE AND BUSINESS

My current situation is quite unique. Since opening our studio, I've had to change the way I work. I now work in the flesh 3–4 days a week in our Mordialloc club in Melbourne, and, at the end of the week, I fly home to Brisbane to be with my fiancé. In Brisbane, I work in my home office, which has proven to be quite beneficial, as I can work on big-picture plans in relative peace and quiet.

After the first year of business, I qualified to be a group fitness and Pilates instructor. It's a fantastic way to connect with members and get a bit of a workout myself. It also means I need to practise my classes, so I'm forced to train – win win! I also do all the Fernwood national challenges and try to attend at least two group classes a week. If I can't find time to get active in my own gym, how can I help new members with their time objections? It's all about leading by example.

"DO OR DO NOT. THERE IS NO TRY."

My old boss used to call me Bulldog. Why? Because once I have an idea or concept or need something done, I hold on until it *is* done, just like a bulldog holds on with its teeth. I believe in fighting for what's right and trusting your instincts regarding whether something will work or not. From there, you must do what it takes to see the project completed, following through to the end, just like we did with the Fernwood Fusion concept. If I didn't come at it like a bulldog, it wouldn't have been the success it was.

Even though running a business can be demanding, it's important to still have fun. Don't forget to talk to people – members and staff – to learn their personal stories. In my experience, taking interest in people and their lives creates a more positive club environment with happy, engaged staff. It's also important to learn all of your members' names. They're trusting you with their health and wellness journeys, so it's the least we can do.

To avoid getting overwhelmed with work, you must learn to *delegate*. You can't do it all. Train people to help with certain tasks so you can focus on areas of the business where you can have the most impact. Running a business is rarely easy, but you *can* make it easier.

When I look back, the studio concept is completely different from when we first started. Essentially, we were willing to learn as we went and make some difficult calls along the way. The goal was to provide an exceptional Fernwood service to our members in a boutique-style environment, and, with bulldog-like effort, we achieved it.

Connect
WITH US

To connect with us and access bonus content and exclusive offers, scan the QR code or follow the link. We look forward to sharing more with you.

www.fernwoodfitness.com.au/womenfittolead

SCAN ME

EVERY SINGLE
PERSON WHO WALKS
THROUGH OUR
DOORS LEAVES
feeling happier
THAN THEY WERE
WHEN THEY ARRIVED.

Brooke & *Danielle*
WOODWORTH LOVELUCK

TWO PATHS, ONE DESTINATION

As sisters, we grew up in an active and sporty family, and both of us always loved going to the gym. We started when we were very young, going with Dad in the mornings before school. The idea of physical exercise was so ingrained in us that we both chose career paths that led us to working in the fitness industry – Brooke worked as a club manager, and Dani became an exercise physiologist.

Brooke originally joined Fernwood as a member in 2009 after returning from an overseas trip a little on the heavy side. At the time, she felt very self-conscious, and the big gyms were far too intimidating, so Fernwood was the obvious choice to help her get back in shape. The environment was so welcoming and non-judgemental. Anyone could go in, do a workout, and not have to worry about what anyone thought of them, which was exactly what she needed.

When the opportunity arose to purchase Fernwood Waurn Ponds, it was a no-brainer for us. We had both dedicated our lives to working in the fitness industry, and owning a club was the next logical step in our careers. Looking back, it was the best decision we could have made.

WE DIDN'T KNOW WHAT WE WERE WALKING INTO

When we took over our Fernwood club in 2019, we had absolutely no idea what was about to hit us. Essentially, we walked into a club that was in much worse condition than we were anticipating. The members and staff were all extremely unhappy with the previous owner and very suss about what we were going to bring to the party. We were, after all, two girls they had never met before.

Those first few weeks were daunting and challenging. However, we came in with a clear vision: to positively impact the lives of as many women in our community as possible by improving their overall health and wellbeing through physical activity, community, and connection. We aimed to create an environment where all women could feel supported, connected, and empowered with confidence to thrive in all areas of their lives. The team quickly bought into this, and we listened to feedback from members and staff and made a positive impact in the club environment.

We made it clear that the value of our club came from our team, and, as franchisees, our first priority was, and still is, to create an environment where every team member felt supported and valued.

BLINDSIDED – WE NEVER SAW IT COMING

Just when we were getting into the groove of being club owners, COVID hit. Never in our wildest dreams could we have imagined a global pandemic practically bringing life to a standstill. When the pandemic hit, the impact it had on us, our families, our members, our staff, and our entire community was beyond belief.

Even so, we were ready for action. There was no way we were going to let a pesky once-in-a-lifetime pandemic jeopardise everything we had worked so hard for, so we did everything in our power to rally our team and community and stay connected. We created Facebook groups, online workouts and fitness classes, and even dropped care packages off to our staff to let them know we were thinking of them. It was these small touches that kept our team connected and enabled us to propel forwards as soon as we were allowed to reopen our doors.

A POSITIVE AND WELCOMING ENVIRONMENT FOR ALL

We believe that if you look after your team members, they will look after your customers. It's a belief we absolutely live and breathe. We love spoiling our team with gifts, coffees, and team events, and we're always asking how to be better leaders to better support our team.

Little gestures can add up to big outcomes. While we know our numbers, they're not our primary focus. We believe that results come from all the little things, including cleanliness, impeccable customer service, and helping our members actually achieve results. We're more customer-focused than profit-driven, and it has helped us create a business that can thrive now and well into the future.

Essentially, we treat our members as if they're coming into our home. When you welcome someone into your home, you want them to feel warm, comfortable, and relaxed. Because it's your home, it's your responsibility. It's no different in business. When a member walks through our doors, whether for the first time or the thousandth, it's our responsibility to make them feel at home.

WORKAHOLISM, PERFECTIONISM, MOTHERHOOD

In recent years, we've both undergone massive transformation and growth through the journey into motherhood and continuing to run a business. When we took over the club, Brooke had a 2-year-old and was seven months pregnant with her second child. She now has three children, Isaac, age 6, Evie, age 4, and Patrick, age 2. Dani is also now a mother to her 18-month-old daughter Izzy, with another one on the way.

As mums of young children, we get pulled in different directions every day, but we both thrive on getting up super early and getting some movement in before the day begins. It helps set us up for the day ahead and ensures that we practise what we preach.

We're both very organised – we have to be! We try our best to have systems in place and plan, plan, plan! It's all about those little 1-percent tasks: making the beds in the morning, prepping and planning the meals for the week, keeping our inboxes under control – the little things that add up to make a big difference. We're also both list lovers. We each have big business planning diaries, which we both use religiously to help remove the little things from the backs of our minds so we can focus on what's in front of us.

We have a confession to make: we're both workaholics. It's a label we've both given to ourselves and to each other. However, having young kids has made it necessary to slow down and focus on other areas of life. Kids grow up so fast, and we're both passionate about spending as much time with ours as possible while, at the same time, being completely present. Sometimes this means answering emails at 10 pm or working weekends, but it's not lost on us just how fortunate we are to have such flexibility around work.

Not only are we workaholics, but we've always been (and probably always will be) perfectionists. In the past, with everything we did, we aimed to get every little detail perfect. However, as our time and energy got further and further stretched to meet the needs of our families and team, we had to question our perfectionist tendencies. We've now (mostly) learnt to accept that sometimes 'done' is better than 'perfect'.

AN HONOUR AND A PRIVILEGE

Working in the health and fitness industry is such a privilege. The impact we have on the women in our community is phenomenal. Every single person who walks through our doors leaves feeling happier than they were when they arrived.

We'll never forget the day we saw one of our members come in, drop her two little ones at creche, do a 20-minute workout, have a shower, wash and dry her hair, make herself a coffee, and have some breakfast. I asked her how she was and if she had much planned for the day, and she shared that this was the only time she would have for herself for the whole day and how she looked forward to coming to the gym so much for this time. She shared that coming in and having this space got her through her darkest days as a new Mum. It really took my breath away.

We're so proud of the fact that we give women the opportunity to breathe and practise just a little self-care. It's what keeps us doing what we do.

Mong Thanh NGUYEN

— PRESTON & EPPING, VICTORIA —

FROM CORPORATE LIFE TO EMPOWERING WOMEN TO SHINE

I've always loved group fitness. Over the years, I tried several different clubs, but none quite felt right. Eventually, I joined Fernwood Preston, and I haven't looked back.

After attending many group fitness classes, I decided that I too could inspire others to love to exercise, so that's when I decided to become a group fitness instructor myself, delivering classes at the Preston club. At the time, I was instructing three classes per week while still working my full-time corporate job. I soon realised that the corporate world wasn't fulfilling my aspirations – I wanted complete autonomy in a career that fulfilled and challenged me. Essentially, I wanted to be a business owner.

When I saw that the Preston club was for sale, I sprang into action, diving into the club's operations and learning what went on behind the scenes. Instantly, I knew my calling was to own a Fernwood club.

UNFORESEEN CHALLENGES OF CLUB OWNERSHIP

When you're a club owner, you're expected to play many roles: sales, maintenance, leadership, day-to-day operations, saving membership cancellations, and so much more. Staff and members look up to you, and they expect you to have all the answers. I've certainly learnt a lot since taking over the Preston club, but I could never know it all.

One of the most important lessons I learnt was that having the right team around you is key to running a successful business. You should have people on your team who want to be there, who are happy for your success, and who want to share in it with you. Having a supportive network around you, both professionally and personally, can help provide clarity, as it means you have access to a variety of opinions. What you think is right isn't always right, no matter how much you want it to be.

When running a business, being a part of a brand is super helpful. You have extra hands and heads to help with strategy and day-to-day operations. For me, learning from other franchisees has been invaluable. If I encounter a problem, chances are another franchisee has already solved it.

For me, the toughest part of running a business was learning to say no and say it with empathy. Initially, I felt awful saying no to staff members; however, I learnt to always consider what was best for the business, even if it meant disappointing someone. As leaders, it's important that we focus on the facts and don't let feelings override logic. If I'm being practical and empathetic, it can make those challenging decisions and conversations a little easier.

WHERE I GOT MY STRONG WORK ETHIC

When my family came to Australia, we didn't have much. My parents worked long hours and didn't spend as much time as they would have liked with me and my brother. Their strong work ethic got them where they are today and taught me the value of hard work.

Some days, I have to do double shifts because a staff member is sick or the club is under-resourced due to leave. The work ethic my parents instilled in me drives me to do those extra hours. Essentially, I'll do whatever it takes to make the business a success and to ensure the operation runs smoothly. Honestly, because I love what I do, I don't mind working long hours (not all the time though!). I see that extra time in the club as an opportunity to connect with members and staff who I might not usually interact with during my normal working day. When you have so much love for what you do, it never feels like work, and getting out of bed every day is a blessing!

Don't get me wrong – running a business can be challenging, but, at the same time, it can be so rewarding. To me, the best part of owning a Fernwood club is that I get to take on multiple roles: front desk worker, cleaner, fitness instructor, leader. Every day, I get to create magic in the club, one way or another.

When I work with my team, I don't like the members knowing who I am. It's my way of showing the team that I'm with them – I'm one of them. One day, after I instructed a class, a member said to me, "Are you new here? I love your classes so much." To her, I was just another fitness instructor, which is exactly how I want it to be. I love being a part of the team, and, generally, there's no reason for the members to know I own the club.

STRIKING A DELICATE BALANCE

As a busy club owner, I've learnt to ensure that my week is always filled with something for me. It's easy to get caught up in running the club and forget to take some me time. Each week, I aim to do at least one reformer Pilates class, spin class, or treadmill run to keep my mind happy. Mental health is important, and I feel it can be achieved when our bodies feel good. Being a group fitness instructor certainly helps me meet my target!

To maintain a good work-life balance, I prefer not to work in the evenings. Instead, I like to come home and cook a yummy dinner for my family. Family dinners are my favourite – they're a time when I get to sit down and connect with my son Tyson and partner David. I also enjoy the occasional cheeky glass of wine – because I deserve it!

On top of everything else, every year, I like to do a development course to keep up to date with the industry. For example, in 2023, I got my reformer Pilates qualification. I'm always looking for ways to expand my knowledge and skill set.

A DREAM MADE REAL

From the moment I began training at the Preston club, I fell in love with the Fernwood brand. When I met Di during the franchisee application process, I quickly understood why Fernwood was such a success.

She took a dream and turned it into an amazing world where women feel safe and happy to train. I'm sure her journey hasn't been easy, but she should be extremely proud of the brand she has built, giving other women who dream the same dream amazing opportunities to thrive as club owners.

In business, every day is a new day, so expect the unexpected and embrace every opportunity to learn and grow. For me, not a single day as a business owner has been the same. Every day brings new connections, new conversations, and new energy – love what you do.

AT THE END OF THE DAY, THIS ISN'T A PRACTICE LIFE –
it's the real deal.

Julie NIXON

— ALBURY, NEW SOUTH WALES —

MAKING EVERYONE FEEL SPECIAL

When I was 10 years old, I was diagnosed with a brain tumour. It was a really difficult time, as I missed out on lots of school, got held back a year, and really struggled with keeping and making friends. From this experience, I knew I wanted to make everyone feel special and wanted, no matter where they came from, what clothes they wore, whether they wore make-up or did their hair. Eventually, I found my calling, although I didn't know it was my calling at first.

In 2010, I became a Les Mills group fitness instructor when my buddy Brooke – who's now an instructor at Ferny Albury – wanted to get her trainer qualification. I didn't actually plan to become an instructor; I mainly wanted to support Brooke, but I loved the classes. In fact, I'd loved the Les Mills workouts since first experiencing them in year 10 PE classes. So, a month after completing my training, I instructed my first class and never looked back. As an instructor, I love seeing people bond, laugh, and encourage and support one another.

When the Fernwood Albury club opened, I began teaching there, and I instantly fell in love with the female-only gym experience. It felt fresh, clean, and super friendly. By day, I was an accountant and a bookkeeper for a GP surgery, and I taught Les Mills classes – pump, sprint, RPM – on either side of my day job.

I loved being in the club, but I'd never considered owning one myself until Ann, the owner of Fernwood Albury, explained that she was selling the club and suggested that I seriously consider investing in it. As accountants do, I examined the financials and saw that there was potential to grow the business. In my mind, I wouldn't just be buying a business; I'd be investing in, running, and growing a business I had immense passion for. *This is going to be fun,* I thought.

MORE THAN A GYM

Fernwood Albury is more than a gym; it's a loving and supportive community where we all look out for each other. To me, the health and fitness benefits members receive at Ferny are just an added bonus. In our club, lifelong friendships and strong support networks are formed.

I've seen ladies lose their lifetime partners, and the support they get at Fernwood is invaluable. For example, a member was really struggling moving forward with her life after losing her husband of over 65 years, so we reached out to the members we knew were close to her to see what we could do to help. We ended up with over 50 members who put their names down to take it in turns to visit her each day. Amazing! This is why I love my job and why I have a smile on my face every day.

During the COVID pandemic, we kept morale up by holding outdoor boot camps, not so much for the workouts but so our members could still socialise. It was a freezing -2°C outside, but that didn't stop people from signing up. To many, it was worth the discomfort, and I was so happy we could bring them all together in such a challenging and uncertain time.

Our club really is a warm and welcoming environment. When I teach my Friday Body Pump class, I usually have a full house (32 participants); however, I always say it's like 32 mothers-in-law, sisters, and aunties all having a great time together. We're all so close. When a new member joins the class, they're quickly whisked away by other members to get set up, have the class explained, and get ready to go. The one quote we constantly hear from new members is, "Why didn't I join earlier?"

All across the Fernwood network, our goal is to empower women to shine by giving them the confidence they need to succeed in all they do. I'm happy to say, it's a goal I see achieved every single day.

TOUGH TIMES LEAD TO BETTER TIMES

When I took over Fernwood Albury in November 2017, my team and I managed to significantly boost our member count. However, when COVID hit, we got knocked right back down – but we didn't stay down. Once the worst of the pandemic had passed, we went right back to work on growing our member base, and it's now bigger and better than ever.

In business, there will always be tough times, and the key to surviving in the long term is to work hard and keep pushing through. As with the pandemic, the tough times won't last forever.

Another key to long-term success is to keep it fresh. You should always be looking for new ways to improve your facilities, stay ahead of the competition, and increase revenue. How can your business evolve? What can you add to make it stand out from the rest? For example, at Fernwood, over the years, we've added FIIT30, sauna, and reformer Pilates. You've got to spend money to make money. Don't do anything cheaply, and invest in the best.

As a club owner, I believe it's super important to be a role model for our members, so I always make time for exercise. Make time, not excuses. If we really want to, most of us can find at least 30 minutes per day to exercise. As well as training in the club, I love cycling, running, hiking – anything outdoors. I'm very introverted, and I love having some 'me time'.

At the end of the day, this isn't a practice life – it's the real deal. So, go out there and get shit done. Embrace each day and squeeze the most out of every second. Be happy, have fun, and enjoy every day. I know it's not always easy. For me, running a business has been tough, don't get me wrong. A lot of blood, sweat, and tears have gone into it but also a lot of laughter, love, excitement, and fun. These are the things that make it all worth while.

Angela
WILLIAMS

— ST KILDA, VICTORIA —

BORN FOR FITNESS

I'm lucky to say that Di is my mother, so I had roots in the fitness industry from a very young age. I was a very energetic kid, and my friends and I were always looking for new things to do outside of our regular sports. We decided to join the gym across the paddock from where we lived, as it was so close, and my good friend from school was dating the son of the owner, so we knew the people running the gym.

Now, back then, gyms were very basic, and the one we joined was a far cry from the beautiful, inviting Fernwood clubs we have now. This gym was in a big, metal shed, no air con, lots of big, scary, blokey equipment and big men, and not much else. No bells, no whistles. It wasn't set up to make women feel comfortable, but do you know what? We didn't care. We were just happy to have something new to do, and it was kinda fun.

As I was such an active child, I'd often go to old-school aerobic classes with Mum, both of us in our leotards, doing the grapevine. I also did lots of different sports. Netball, softball, indoor soccer, judo, squash, badminton – honestly, there wasn't much I didn't do. I also rode my bike everywhere; I rarely stopped moving. No doubt, my active childhood shaped me into the person I am today.

MY FERNWOOD JOURNEY – FROM RECEPTIONIST TO CLUB OWNER

In the 90s, when I returned to Australia after seven years overseas, I began my Fernwood journey working reception. I then moved into sales, which led to management.

From day one, Fernwood was a fun and positive environment to work in, and I quickly grew to love every aspect of the fitness industry. I'm naturally a people person, so I really enjoyed the social side and meeting so many wonderful women. As a bonus, working in the club had a very positive effect on my personal health, fitness, and attitude.

After working in several Fernwood clubs, I moved to the support office in the CBD, working in operations. In that role, I assisted clubs all across Australia to improve their businesses, focusing on cash flow, expenses, club presentation, and team management. I enjoyed the role so much that I soon asked myself, *Why not open my own club?* – which I did, opening a club in Prahran, Victoria in 2002.

When I first opened my club, I didn't fully understand how much I needed to know as a business owner. I was a bit naive, but I had taken the plunge, and I was ready and willing to learn on the go.

I was so fortunate to have some amazing mentors along the way, from other franchisees to the team at the support office that I was working alongside. That's the great thing about being in a franchise – you don't have to go it alone. You have the support of people who have already done it or are currently doing it, so they understand your situation perfectly and can offer great advice. Without all the support I received, that first year could have been very overwhelming. Fortunately, I survived and, over time, grew more comfortable in my role as a business owner. I'm still learning now – it never stops.

After five years at Prahran, I decided to move my club to St Kilda. It was a brilliant decision that I've never regretted, even if it came with a new set of challenges. St Kilda is a very transient suburb, full of backpackers and travellers, so we needed to adapt to accommodate short-term visitors, who quickly became a large part of our club. Because Prahran and St Kilda are so close, I was able to move many of my members over to the new club – a big bonus. Although the move was stressful, I've never looked back. I love my St Kilda club and the St Kilda ladies.

HOW TO STAY SANE WHILE RUNNING A BUSINESS

I've now been in business for over two decades – hard to believe, as it has gone so fast – and I'm still frequently confronted with new and interesting challenges. It's an unavoidable part of business, and it keeps things interesting. When challenges do arise, you must find a way to overcome them – and you always do!

Over the years, I've learnt that even the most seemingly insurmountable obstacles can be overcome, every single time.

There's no problem that doesn't have a solution. Every time you go through these, you grow as a person and a business owner, and it strengthens your skill set and confidence. Never be afraid to ask for help.

I'll admit, initially, working in a business that is open 24/7 was overwhelming. The workload felt constant, and I struggled to switch off. However, I soon learnt that I couldn't focus on the business 24 hours a day. Enjoying free time for yourself is essential to long-term success, happiness, and wellbeing. I live a very full life outside of work, which is essential to my happiness. Each day, I try to leave my work at the club (as much as I can), which not only allows me to switch off but also helps me stay focused when I am working, as I'm refreshed and ready to go.

I once heard someone – I don't remember who – say the key is to work 'on' your business and not 'in' it. I'm still trying to master that one, but I know it's essential to make time to analyse your business, practise strategic thinking, get creative, and give your mind space to troubleshoot and project plans for the future. If you are 'in' your business too much, you'll likely end up chasing your tail, not setting yourself clear goals and achieving them, not solving problems, and not seeing the whole picture. For me, taking a step back from constantly being in the business has been an important part of running a successful club.

To avoid feeling stressed or overwhelmed, I do a couple of short meditations each day, which has made a huge difference to my attitude. When your to-do list seems never-ending, it's so important to stop, calm the mind, and reset occasionally.

I also make it a priority to exercise daily, as it helps clear my mind and boost energy levels. For me, a morning workout is the best way to start the day, followed by walking the dog, and maybe some yoga or Pilates in the evening. I consider my workouts to be a part of my job; our members love seeing us, as team members, working out in the club and participating in classes. It shows that we believe in what we do. We walk the talk, and it's a great way to interact with members. I encourage the entire team to work out in the club, as it also boosts their happiness and productivity. A healthy person is a happy person.

Essentially, your team members are the core of your business, and they must be treated with the utmost respect, enjoy what they do, and feel appreciated. It will make your business run so much better if you've created a positive and happy team culture. Everyone needs a good work-life balance so they can come into work, give their all, and then switch off at the end of the day. We all need time for ourselves.

Outside of work, I love seeing live music with friends, playing tennis, and paddleboarding. I enjoy many creative hobbies, such as painting, pottery, and playing guitar, and I love being in nature. Travel is another of my passions. My partner Mark and I take regular trips away to experience different cultures. All of this keeps me well-balanced, happy, and loving what I do!

IT'S EASY TO GET
CAUGHT UP IN
THE CHALLENGES,
BUT MAINTAINING A
positive outlook
AND DOING OUR
BEST IN ALL
CIRCUMSTANCES ARE
FOUNDATIONAL TO
our approach.

Claire & Sallyann
DICKENS NORMINGTON

— CAIRNLEA, CHIRNSIDE PARK, CRAIGIEBURN,
SYDENHAM, TULLAMARINE & TARNEIT, VICTORIA —

A FAMILY AFFAIR

Becoming Fernwood club owners has been a wild ride, especially since it's a family affair. We've faced our fair share of challenges, surviving the 2008 global financial crisis and navigating the 2020 pandemic. But, honestly, the most unique challenge has been managing the ups and downs while keeping our family dynamics intact. Fernwood has been a rock during tough times, offering support that goes beyond just business.

To tackle any family-run business pitfalls, we've set clear guidelines and divvied up responsibilities. It's like having our own playbook that everyone's on board with. And, to keep things real, we've made a rule: no talking shop at the dinner table. It's our way of making sure work doesn't take over our personal lives.

Sure, it has been a rollercoaster, but it has also been incredibly rewarding. The surprises and challenges have taught us resilience, adaptability, and the importance of the Fernwood community. It's not just a business; it has become a part of who we are and how we navigate life's twists and turns.

A SHARED JOURNEY OF CHALLENGES AND TRIUMPHS

The most rewarding aspect of running a Fernwood club is witnessing women tap into their true potential and observing their growth in the fitness industry. It's incredibly fulfilling to see members transition into happier, healthier, more fulfilling lives by achieving their health and fitness goals. We are also proud of and driven by the members who transition into staff roles and progress through various key positions, from becoming personal trainers and group fitness instructors to ultimately stepping into roles as club managers or even club owners. For us, being a part of these journeys is the best part of the job.

One particularly inspirational story involves a member who started as a fitness enthusiast and, with our support and mentorship, eventually became a certified personal trainer. Watching her confidence skyrocket and witnessing the positive impact she had on others in the club was truly heartwarming. Eventually, she took on a managerial role and is now thriving as a leader within the Fernwood community.

In our Fernwood community, the bonds forged extend beyond the typical employer-employee relationship. It's like we've become one big extended family, navigating not only the highs of individual successes but also supporting each other through the collective journey of challenges and triumphs. We share in the joy of personal achievements, from a club member reaching their fitness goals to a staff member excelling in their career path. It's not just about the business; it's also about celebrating the milestones, big and small, that shape our shared experience.

Whether it's assisting a colleague with a challenging task or celebrating birthdays and achievements together, there's a genuine care for one another's wellbeing. This familial atmosphere not only makes the workplace more enjoyable but also contributes to the overall positive environment that defines Fernwood clubs.

So, beyond the inspirational stories, the real magic lies in the connections we've built – a Fernwood family that cheers each other on through the highs and provides a pillar of support during the lows. It's this unity that makes running a Fernwood club not just a business venture but a shared journey with a community that feels like home.

THE BLUEPRINT FOR A THRIVING BUSINESS

As club owners, we function as the air traffic controllers of our club, ensuring a smooth operation every day. Over the years, we've learnt so many critical lessons that have helped our club thrive.

Firstly, for us, member happiness is a top priority. It's not just a business strategy; it's a philosophy that has profound ripple effects. Happy members not only stay longer, contributing to business stability, but they also achieve better results. Additionally, satisfied members become advocates, spreading positive word-of-mouth, which is a potent marketing tool. Prioritising member happiness creates a healthy life cycle, fostering a positive feedback loop that fuels the growth and sustainability of the business.

Secondly, team happiness is another top priority for us. Your team forms the backbone of your business. Recognising the direct link between team happiness and member satisfaction is crucial. A content and motivated team not only directly contributes to member happiness but also shapes the overall culture and atmosphere in the club. If your team is happy, that positivity naturally extends to the members, creating a welcoming and vibrant environment. Investing in team wellbeing is an investment in the core of your business – the people who drive its success.

Thirdly, cash is queen. Understanding the dynamics of cash flow has been a critical lesson for us. This insight proved invaluable during the global financial crisis and the challenges presented by the COVID-19 pandemic. Recognising the ebb and flow of finances ensures the business's resilience during economic uncertainties, providing a buffer and strategic flexibility to navigate through tough times.

Fourthly, each working day, we take the necessary steps to ensure that our club is thriving and continues to thrive well into the future. Our checklist for a successful day looks like this:

1. **Review the day ahead** – Get a clear picture of what's in store for the day.
2. **Set a plan** – Establish priorities and tasks for the day.
3. **Set expectations** – Communicate goals and expectations to the team.

4. **Inspect and review results** – Evaluate progress and outcomes.

5. **Rinse and repeat** – Continuously refine and optimise our processes.

Finally, a key principle we adhere to is 'avoid distractions'. It's easy to be enticed by shiny new ideas or projects, but we resist the allure until our daily plan is solid. It's similar to a scuba diver planning a dive meticulously. If she gets distracted by pretty fish and strays off course, she risks running out of oxygen. Staying focused on our fundamentals ensures that our daily operations remain efficient and effective.

DEFINING THE LINE BETWEEN WORK AND DOWNTIME

Maintaining a work-life balance is undoubtedly a challenge, especially with access to work at our fingertips and the ability to work from home blurring the line between work and personal time. The temptation to work around the clock is always present, fuelled by the constant demands.

To tackle this, we prioritise switching off. It's crucial to delineate between what's truly urgent and what can wait until the next day. Clearly defining priorities allows us to create boundaries, ensuring that work doesn't encroach excessively on personal time. Whether it's spending quality moments with family, pursuing personal interests, or simply taking a breather, these moments of disconnection are vital for recharging and maintaining a sense of balance.

Acknowledging that there will always be tasks to complete and recognising the limits of what can be achieved in a day are essential steps towards striking a balance. It's an ongoing process of setting boundaries, making conscious choices, and valuing personal time as much as professional commitments. Ultimately, finding equilibrium is a unique journey for each entrepreneur, and, for us, it involves a constant dance between dedication to our business and cherishing moments of relaxation and personal fulfilment.

Staying positive is a key belief we live by. We strive to find the silver linings in every situation. It's easy to get caught up in the challenges, but maintaining a positive outlook and doing our best in all circumstances are foundational to our approach. In the dynamic world of business, this belief not only keeps us resilient but also contributes to fostering a vibrant and uplifting environment within our Fernwood community.

Nicole
WESTAWAY

ACHIEVING SUCCESS
WITHOUT THE STRESS

Before becoming a Fernwood franchisee, I worked on a cattle station in the Northern Territory with my husband Nathan and his family. When we sold the station, we relocated to Darwin, and I joined the Fernwood gym where my sister Shaye worked.

The more time I spent in the club, the more I realised that my values aligned with those of the company. I could see myself running my own Fernwood club one day. In fact, I could see myself running the very Darwin club I was attending. Unfortunately, it wasn't for sale, but that didn't stop me from discussing the idea with Shaye and approaching the owner with a proposition to purchase the club. To our surprise, the owner agreed to sell, and, six months later, Shaye, her husband Phil, Nathan, and I became the proud owners of Fernwood Darwin.

BUSINESS STOPS FOR NOTHING

When we purchased our club, the word 'failure' wasn't in my vocab. In my mind, success was all but guaranteed. I was too driven to fail. Even so, we experienced many challenges and surprises along the way.

The early days were incredibly chaotic and challenging. Not only did I have to learn how to run a new business, but I also had two young children – Chloe, 5 years old, and Logan, almost 2. To throw a spanner in the works, Nathan was charged by a bull at a rodeo and ended up in intensive care. It was touch and go for a while, but I had to stay strong. *I have to get my thoughts together,* I thought. *I have to be strong and positive. I can't let the kids know how unwell their dad is.* During this time, I was so lucky to have a supportive family to help look after our children while I sat with Nathan in the hospital. To help me maintain my strength and good health, I began working with a naturopath. It's something I still do to this day.

I quickly learnt that business stops for no one, and juggling running the club with being there for my husband wasn't easy. Thankfully, in the end, Nathan pulled through, and so did the business. Without a doubt, that challenging time strengthened my character and helped me build resilience. I'm much stronger now for having gone through it.

To give our club the best chance of success, I engaged a business coach, who I still meet with monthly. We combine walking and coaching, which increases my creative thinking.

The coaching includes reflection, acknowledgement of achievements, discussion of challenges and opportunities, and setting new goals.

I also focus on self-development, including improving my communication skills through engaging with others and active listening. Consequently, I've built many authentic business relationships, undertaken transparent negotiations, and respectfully managed tricky situations in a calm and professional manner. I'm a very curious person, and I'm always looking for ways to learn and grow.

WHEN STRESS GETS DANGEROUS

I've grown a lot since becoming a Fernwood franchisee. When we first purchased the club, I worked at 100 miles an hour, was highly driven, a 'yes' person, high on adrenaline, and I would forget to come up for breath. As I soon discovered, my approach to work wasn't sustainable.

One evening, when I was sitting at the dinner table with Nathan and the kids, my arm went completely numb. *Am I having a stroke?* Understandably, I was freaked out. Because I didn't want to freak anyone else out, I excused myself from the dinner table and went to the bedroom to figure out what the hell was going on with my body. Suddenly, I felt an overwhelming shortness of breath, which made me panic even more. I rushed back out to the dining room and explained what was happening. Clearly, I needed to go to the hospital.

At the hospital, I had an ECG, and the staff thoroughly checked me over. As it turned out, the cause of the numbness was stress, and the remedy was a series of nerve stretches, which a fabulous doctor guided me through. Within 45 minutes, the numbness had faded, and I could feel my arm again.

The event made me realise I was burnt out, and I decided to place more importance on managing my mind, body, and soul for better health. I started doing yoga, meditation, and breathwork. I began living my life with a focus on my and my family's physical and mental wellbeing, which flowed on to our members and the business.

With a renewed focus on myself and the gym, I developed an increased awareness of what many of our members were truly seeking – increased wellness, just like me – which led to me providing a more holistic wellness approach in the club. Essentially, I learnt to control my stress levels while helping others do the same.

WE ARE ONE

Running a Fernwood club fills me with immense satisfaction. Why wouldn't it? I get to create a beautiful space and community for women, a space where we have each other's best interests at heart.

Every time I walk into our club, I feel this incredible energy and happiness that puts a smile on my face. Fernwood Darwin is a place of kindness, laughter, and support. The team and I have worked so hard to build such an incredible community of diverse women, and we're very protective of our space. At Fernwood Darwin, we are one.

I'm so proud to be a Fernie Darwin girl!

Michelle
CALDWELL

THE MARATHON MINDSET

Growing up, I always hoped to have an interesting career with opportunities to learn, grow, and do rewarding work. Both of my parents worked hard all throughout their careers, and I got my work ethic from them.

Throughout my career, I have had some wonderful work opportunities, where I was always learning, both on the job and through formal education.

I had my first gym experience in 2001 when I saw a personal trainer – and it changed my life in more ways than I could have reasonably expected! From that point on, my husband Ric and I fully committed to fitness. In 2012, I completed my first marathon, and, in 2013, Ric competed in the World Masters Games in Italy. As fitness enthusiasts, when we began looking for a business to buy, we quickly looked to Fernwood for opportunities.

ASSEMBLING THE DREAM TEAM

Ric and I had worked together previously and liked the idea of combining our skills to run our own business. I had been a member of Fernwood for nine years, and I loved the idea of creating a space where women could train in a supportive community without judgement.

In 2014, we bought our club, beginning the chapter of owning a family business. Because we came from outside the fitness industry, running a Fernwood club came with a steep learning curve. Thankfully, we were part of a network that was happy to support us as new franchisees, and we built a team that focused on supporting our members. We made up for our lack of industry experience with our business skills, attitude towards learning, and willingness to adapt. For instance, if you understand financials (Ric is an accountant), strategy, and leadership, you can learn the rest as you go or find the necessary skills within your team. Understanding financials is a big one. It's easy to overspend on things that don't bring a return on investment. Plus, there are always unexpected expenses, so it's really important to keep a close eye on the figures. Thankfully, I have Ric for that, and he's the one who holds me back when I want to overspend on the club.

As a club owner, it helped that I started my Fernwood journey as a member, as it allows me to run our club from a member's perspective. Even now, I still draw on my experience as a member when making important decisions. After all, our members are the reason we get out of bed each day.

Since becoming a club owner, I've loved working with women who are passionate about supporting our members to reach their goals. Leading a great team of people who are passionate about what they do is one of the best aspects of owning a club. We've got a strong culture of learning within our team, and it's rewarding to see our team members master new skills and take the next steps in their roles. I love that we're able to give them these opportunities.

As a bonus, I get to work with my daughter Rose and my sister Tam. Tam and I look a lot alike, so it's common for members to get us confused – it happens most days. When members mix us up, we have some strange conversations, and they always end in a laugh.

Recently, we employed a manager, Connie, to job share with me so I could continue studying and training for the 2024 New York Marathon. The freedom to structure the team to support my life is something I don't take for granted.

In business and in life, it's important to find your tribe. Ideally, you should surround yourself with people who have a can-do attitude and positive mindset, who will be honest with you and tell you what you need to hear, whose opinions you trust, who want the best for you, who want to see you succeed. Why would you accept anything less?

THE PERKS OF GYM OWNERSHIP

Recently, I completed a radio interview where the journalist jokingly asked me if I pay for a gym membership at our club. I said, "No, actually, I don't. When I train, I like to walk around like I own the place," which got the appropriate laugh.

Not only do I have limitless access to a fully equipped gym – no membership required! – but I also buy equipment for the club that I want to use for my own strength training. It's just one of the perks of owning a gym. Of course, new equipment doesn't just benefit me; it also benefits our members.

BE CURIOUS AND OPEN TO LEARNING

Continuous learning is a big part of our success as Fernwood club owners. I don't know everything, but I am curious about many things. As a part of my ongoing commitment to education, I completed a Bachelor of Exercise Sport Science, which has proved useful in my role as a club owner. There's so much important research happening right now that will impact the programs we deliver in the future. Research is really exciting, and I love keeping up to date with the latest. As club owners, we have a responsibility to our members to keep our skills current. There's always something to learn, something important that we don't already know.

In business, a marathon mindset is essential. To succeed, you must have staying power, and you must be able to manage your time and energy. Just like running a marathon, running a business requires resilience, perseverance, and an unwavering commitment to the task at hand.

Kristen
BARLING

WHEN HARDSHIP, PASSION, AND COMMITMENT MEET

Although I grew up in the country and was physically active, I never really played sport or had any interest in exercise. I had a bit of a rough childhood, which led to very low self-confidence, extreme feelings of sadness, and me developing bulimia in my teenage years.

After finishing school, to escape life, I joined the Air Force. Due to my childhood, the discipline required for recruit training didn't bother me; however, my poor physical fitness meant I almost didn't make it through. After failing the physical fitness test several times, I finally scraped through – just. From there, I moved on to my trade training and was eventually posted to Darwin.

Due to my breast size, I was experiencing multiple issues, ranging from back and shoulder problems to struggling with weapons handling, running, and low self-esteem. I was constantly trying every diet or diet pill out there to lose weight, and I still struggled with bulimia. At age 21, I was finally approved to undergo breast reduction surgery – and it completely changed my life.

After my breast reduction, I fell in love with exercise to the point where it became an addiction. Over time, I developed an unhealthy relationship with physical activity, often forcing myself to exercise while sick or injured. The once-positive change in my life had become a serious problem.

I continued to suffer with mental health issues, including depression, self-harm, and suicidal thoughts. However, I pushed through, serving in the Air Force for five years before discharging to pursue my new passion for fitness.

IT COULD HAVE BEEN THE END

I had been a personal trainer and group fitness instructor for almost a decade when I had the opportunity to buy Fernwood Salisbury. I was petrified; I had no idea how to run a club, but, as is my style, I went all in. If someone had told my teenage self that I would own a gym when I was older, she would have thought they were crazy. However, in 2012, I officially became the owner of Fernwood Salisbury.

Unfortunately, soon after buying the business, I experienced a very emotional long-term relationship break-up, which led to the rapid deterioration of my mental health. During this time, I was diagnosed with cervical cancer, and, overwhelmed by everything happening in my life, I attempted suicide. Thankfully, I was unsuccessful.

After a successful surgery, I realised it was time to make some serious life changes. I never wanted to return to that suicidal state, because I truly believed I wouldn't survive it again.

A COMPLETE COMMITMENT

Diving headfirst into my new role as a club owner, I completed course after course, upskilling in every way possible. While I had found my passion, it took me several more years to truly improve my wellbeing. No one knew I was suffering from an eating disorder and severe depression. I was extremely good at hiding it all, even from loved ones. During this time, I was training intensely and even completed five ironman distance triathlons and a bunch of half-ironman triathlons.

I eventually committed myself to doing everything in my power to improve my physical and mental health. I wasn't ready to talk to anyone about my challenges, so I began reading books, doing self-reflection and journaling, and I committed to a full year of practising gratitude every single day. I devoted myself to building self-respect, self-love, and finding joy in life. Now, I always find gratitude in life, no matter what's happening. No matter how challenging my day has been, I always journal at the end of it, listing at least five things I'm grateful for. Due to years of overtraining, I was suffering from a disc extrusion and was told I needed to give up exercise permanently. It was advice I couldn't accept. I became plant-based, dedicated myself to rehabilitation, and managed to heal my back, which meant I could return to high-impact classes and weightlifting.

At a certain point, I realised it had been over six months since my bulimia had surfaced. It has now been many years since I've had a bulimic episode, and, although I've had some down moments, my mental health is much better than it was. I now stop exercising when I'm sick or injured, and I've developed a healthy mental relationship with nutrition.

LEARNING TO ROLL WITH IT

After many years of trying, I managed to heal my body enough to fall pregnant at age 37, having my little miracle baby. I now have two beautiful children, and, although I recently became a single parent, I'm the happiest and most confident I've ever been.

In 2023, I finally built up the confidence and self-belief to compete in a bodybuilding competition, something I had wanted to do for a long time but was always too scared to try. I plan to keep competing, proud to be a strong, muscular, confident, and powerful woman.

I love and am passionate about what I do. In my role as a club owner, it's about being flexible and knowing that the scales will continue to tip one way or another. I just need to roll with it. Sometimes, I need to take time off for my kids, for myself, or I must immerse myself in work, and that's okay.

I've now been a personal trainer and fitness instructor for almost two decades, and my passion for the industry and the Fernwood brand is stronger than ever. Helping other women improve their lives, build confidence, and love themselves and their lives is something I can see myself doing for many years to come.

Ultimately, I followed my passion, and it led to the happiest, most fulfilling point in my life so far. When it comes to anything worth doing, don't be scared to fail. Be scared to not even try.

YOUR TEAM *will respond* **TO YOUR LEADERSHIP, VALUES, AND ATTITUDE, AND YOUR** *business culture* **WILL EITHER MAKE OR BREAK YOUR WORK ENVIRONMENT AND THE OVERALL** *customer experience.*

Chloe
FIDOW

A DREAMER AT HEART

Looking back, when I think about my character, I understand that my childhood and parents played a huge part in shaping who I am today. I was incredibly lucky to grow up in a very loving, nurturing, and encouraging family, where home was our sanctuary and our parents believed in us and supported us wholeheartedly. This foundation of unconditional support gave me the confidence, self-esteem, and discipline to follow my passions and pursue my goals.

My first real taste of success came from dance, which I participated in from an early age. As part of an incredible dance community, I won numerous awards over the years, creating a strong sense of accomplishment. I quickly developed the mentality that whatever I set my mind to, I could achieve.

So, with that drive that was deeply ingrained in me, when the opportunity arose to become a co-owner of a Fernwood Fitness club at age 19, I pursued it without hesitation.

AN AMBITIOUS FIVE-YEAR PLAN

I began working in the health and fitness industry in 2004, and I started work at Fernwood Beverly Hills, NSW in 2005 at age 18 as a member motivator. I immediately fell in love with the brand and all it stood for.

The first franchisee I worked for asked about my five-year plan. Me being me, I answered, "I'd like to own my own Fernwood club within five years." Yep, I was a dreamer at heart. In fact, I still am!

After moving back home to Queensland, I enjoyed a couple of years learning alongside other experienced trainers and franchisees. I was the personal training coordinator at Fernwood Capalaba when the club came up for sale in 2007 – it was the opportunity I'd been waiting for!

I loved our team, our members, and the job, so I went for it. Without hesitation, a colleague and I put forward joint interest, and, with the incredible support of my parents, I purchased the business in partnership and became the co-owner of Fernwood Capalaba before my 20th birthday, putting me well ahead of my five-year plan.

HARD TIMES CAN EITHER MAKE OR BREAK A BUSINESS

As a personal trainer and group fitness instructor, my focus was initially on the fitness side of the business. However, approximately one year in, the global financial crisis (GFC) hit, which impacted our business and many others. While it was an incredibly challenging time, I learnt many invaluable skills and with determination, self-taught business acumen, resilience, a strong why, and lots of support, we got through it.

The GFC wasn't the last big event that would challenge us. In 2020, we took another hit when the COVID pandemic struck. However, remembering the lessons of the past, we rebuilt quickly and even expanded into additional tenancies, upgraded our facilities, added reformer Pilates and HYPOXI to our services, grew our team, revenue, and profits, and I'm proud to say I became the sole owner of the business.

In business, many things will be out of your control. However, that's no reason to accept your business going backwards during difficult times. Adapt, adjust, think outside of the square. With the right attitude and marketing, you can reach many different markets that are waiting for you to share what you do best.

MY TOUGHEST LIFE CHALLENGE

Although I had overcome some tough challenges in business, the hardest, saddest, most pivotal moment in my life was when my brother Dean suddenly passed away at age 37 from a heart attack. Life as I knew it would never be the same.

Dean was the person I would turn to for advice on my long drives home from work. He was someone I admired, right from when I was a little girl all the way through to adulthood. He was unapologetically himself and lived each moment to the fullest. His passing drove home the reality that each day is a gift and we should look after our physical and mental health and spend quality time with the people we love, doing the things we love, pursuing our dreams, and experiencing all life has to offer.

I miss Dean immensely. His passing also gave me a strong sense of purpose to build a business that afforded me and my family a good work-life balance, with a passive income stream. Owning a now-established business is an incredible way to achieve this, and I'm glad we sacrificed so much in the early years, as I now have the privilege to share the rewards with those who supported me.

BUILDING MY DREAM LIFE

Since becoming a Fernwood franchisee, I've also become a mother, which has given me even more purpose to create a life for our kids that grants them the same opportunities I had. I want to give them experiences that will become lifelong memories.

I'm incredibly lucky to have autonomy over my time. My husband and I raise our two beautiful children together, working as a team to ensure we balance family and business. I'm so passionate about being able to have the flexibility to balance mum life and business life, never having to miss moments like school events, play dates, or anything else that's important to my kids.

Without our incredible club manager Michellie, I'd struggle to achieve such freedom and flexibility. She's an integral part of our business and, having been with us for 14 years, is more like family. Over the years, we've grown the club and have a fantastic team behind us so we can service our members and achieve growth each day, with or without me. We've put the right people, systems, and operations in place so I can now spend my time on the business rather than in it every day.

When I am in the club, I enjoy speaking with our members and the team. I love the energy of our club! You can walk in and instantly feel the uplifting energy and warmth that comes with a strong sense of community. From the friendships formed in the members lounge to the high-energy group fitness studio, the feeling is infectious. I'm especially proud of our team members and how they show up every day, with 100 percent commitment to our business, their profession, and our members. Really, it filters down from the top. Your team will respond to your leadership, values, and attitude, and your business culture will either make or break your work environment and the overall customer experience.

Our team really is amazing, and it has been incredible to have our club win several awards over the years, including Cell IQ club of the year, reformer Pilates club of the year, as well as local awards, including best small business in the Redlands and fitness retailer of the year. These recognitions of our team's hard work fill me with immense pride.

IF YOU TRUST
IN YOURSELF
AND YOUR CORE
BELIEFS, YOU
WILL ALWAYS
shine through.

Sylvia
BALEN

— BANKSTOWN, SEVEN HILLS & LIVERPOOL,
NEW SOUTH WALES —

DISCOVERING THE FERNWOOD WAY

When I was 27 years old, I began working as a personal trainer and group fitness instructor in the Parramatta branch. I quickly grew accustomed to the Fernwood way of supporting women to achieve their health and fitness goals. Once I reached my late 30s, I decided it was time to move into ownership.

During the process of becoming a franchisee, I met with Di at the Novotel Sydney. I found her to be so down-to-earth, sensible, and honest, and she gave great advice that I still use today – support and nurture your staff.

Previously, I worked in key management roles at Lifestyle Fitness and Goodlife Health, so I had experience running clubs on a day-to-day basis. Becoming a Fernwood franchisee felt like a natural progression.

SETTING YOURSELF UP FOR SUCCESS

When you're running a business, the challenges are endless. For me, one major challenge was learning to navigate the different personalities and generational characteristics of my staff. To effectively lead my team, I had to overcome all communication barriers and be capable of talking through issues in an open and transparent manner.

Being open and honest is important, as is being open to feedback – the good and the bad. Over the years, the feedback I've received has helped shape my beliefs and ethics. If I had ignored it, I wouldn't be where I am today. I also believe in supporting your key managers in their education so they're capable of making important decisions to keep the business running smoothly. Granting my managers the freedom to make key decisions with my consultation has helped them grow in their roles and has strengthened our relationship.

Ultimately, there's always more to learn, from your staff, colleagues, business partners, everyone around you. Never be afraid to ask for advice.

GAINING PURPOSE AND CONTROL

As a Fernwood club owner, I love that I'm in control of my own livelihood. I get to run my business on my terms and at my pace. If you trust in yourself and your core beliefs, you will always shine through. Why? Because your inner voice speaks the truth.

I also love that I get to help women on their health and fitness journeys, something I've been doing now for many years. I recall one particular member who had been diagnosed with brain cancer. After joining the club, I saw her go from depression to being a strong woman who beat the disease and went on to become a personal trainer herself. Our members are truly inspirational.

Personally, I train every day without fail. I enjoy it, and it sets a good example for our members. I believe we should all give ourselves two hours each day to do whatever we like. For me, that happens to be bikini/physique bodybuilding. Training gives me the clarity I need to get through the day. I also ensure that I plan a 2–3-month overseas vacation during the Australian winter, when it's usually quiet in the clubs. I feel so fortunate to be in a position where this is possible.

IF YOU BELIEVE
IN YOURSELF,
back yourself.
YOU'LL BE
AMAZED AT WHAT
you can achieve.

Danni
WHITAKER

— SHEPPARTON & YARRAVILLE, VICTORIA —

HELPING OTHERS SHINE

While studying a Bachelor of Applied Science/Health and Nutrition at Deakin University, I worked at Fernwood Preston and Epping as a personal trainer. During my time there, I loved helping ladies with their health and fitness goals. I would often work from 5 am, have an afternoon break, and return for the evening clients. At one point, I was training 90 ladies a week. I soon fell in love with the business, the model, and the safe environment Fernwood is for so many women.

When my father, a property developer, told me he had enquired about opening our own Fernwood club in a premises he had acquired, I was only 22 years old. I was shocked and nervous at the proposal, but I knew my father could see how much I loved the Fernwood way. I would often come home and sell the products to my family, so he knew the passion was there.

Friends often describe me as someone who "enjoys a challenge" – and they're right. Although the idea of opening a club was daunting, there was no way I could pass on the opportunity, so, in 2004, we opened our first club, growing to over 1000 beautiful members within three months.

BIG MOVE, BIG CHANGES

In 2016, I moved to regional Victoria, and my husband and I took over the Shepparton club.

For me, running a metro Melbourne club then coming to regional Victoria was a big change. The market was completely different, as was the community. Because I took over an existing club, it took some team members by surprise when I, fuelled by knowledge and passion, made some rapid changes. I wanted to make sure the members and staff had the best of Fernwood – there was no time to waste!

As a club owner, I focus heavily on my team, setting them up for success in every way possible. Your team is everything. If you haven't yet, find your people. Fill your bus with those who share your vision. Find people who can complement your strengths and bolster your weaknesses. I have the pleasure of helping develop many young girls' skills and build their confidence. If they leave me to follow their dreams, which happens now and then, I feel pride in the support I gave them. I love helping others shine, and, at the end of the day, I'm only as good as my team.

ADAPT OR GET LEFT BEHIND

Being a part of Fernwood for two decades, I've seen the company evolve into what it is today. I love that we embrace new concepts and are always trying to better our clubs to help support our teams and members along their journeys.

In the fitness industry, the landscape is constantly changing, so, if we want to stay relevant, we must embrace new ideas and never be scared to make changes. When I first met Di in 2004, she was as passionate then as she is today. She inspires me with her business drive, her vision, and willingness to adapt to stay ahead of the game, keeping us the number one women's health club year after year.

LIFE'S SMALL JOYS

As a club owner, there's no better feeling than when a member walks into my office to share her journey and how wonderful her life has been since joining Fernwood. Every day, I get the opportunity to change someone's life, and watching so many members connect, laugh, and catch up for coffee fills me with joy.

To support myself and inspire our members, I practise what I preach. I've always loved staying fit, and I train regularly in my clubs, which I think members and staff love to see. I train in all areas, living and breathing the Fernwood experience, which helps me keep my club looking and feeling its best. I also do some personal training outside of the club to give myself some 'me time'. As much as I love training in my club, I realised that exercise is really important for my mental health, and I needed to find a space for me outside of my workplace.

Since losing my father to a sudden illness in 2019, I've learnt to appreciate the small things in life. Losing my support person had a big impact on my life. My father believed I had what it took at 22 to open a successful Fernwood club, and, for that, I'll be forever grateful. If you believe in yourself, back yourself. You'll be amazed at what you can achieve.

I've also learnt not to sweat all of life's small problems. What I don't get done today will be there tomorrow. I have two children, and time is precious. Throughout my career, I've always scheduled time outside of work for family. My accountant once said, "Take a week out to disconnect a few times a year. It will allow you to reset and be stronger when you return." It was great advice. When I am away from the club, I love being active with my kids. Bike riding, hiking, paddleboarding – it doesn't matter what we're doing, as long as we're together and having fun.

Andrea & Kristy
MACKEAN JOHNSON

DRIVEN BY FIRM VALUES

When the opportunity arose to purchase the Bellerive Fernwood Fitness club, we already had 15 years of gym management experience and were ready for a new challenge. We had previously discussed the concept of a female-only fitness club, and we were thrilled to be a part of something so big and well-recognised that offered a high standard of service to all women.

Although the transition from operating as independent gym owners to being a part of a franchise was challenging, overall, it was a worthwhile and profitable experience. We've now been Fernwood franchisees for over two decades, and we haven't looked back. However, we couldn't have had such success and longevity without strong values grounded in Christian faith.

NEVER COMPROMISE

We operate our club with integrity and fairness – two very important values to us. Faith in the gospel of Jesus Christ is the bedrock of our worldview, and our belief systems are pivotal in the way we live our lives and run our business. We're early to rise, and we plan, plan, and then plan some more, with our eyes always on the long-term goal. Never sacrifice a long-term gain for a short-term fix.

When it comes to our beliefs, we never compromise. We never bend to passing trends to the detriment of our values. The key in business and in life is to know who you are and to understand your product and its corporate identity. Through this understanding, we were able to create a strong club identity and establish our relevance in the local community, creating an ideal environment for members, staff, franchisees, and franchisor. While you can't please everyone all of the time, you should aim to please most of them most of the time.

People are the wealth of our business. It's always a delight to see so many ladies' lives change through Fernwood. We've been a part of so many stories, so many lives, and it's an honour and a privilege to play a personal role in so many transformations. The numerous testimonials we see and receive, which the whole Fernwood family contributes to, is testament to our commitment to our members and our values. Their stories are truly inspirational.

A HANDS-ON EXPERIENCE

It's not just our members who inspire and motivate us each day. Di has always been hands-on in her business and a strong supporter of women in business, which we appreciate.

Before becoming franchisees, we mainly knew her by reputation. Once we began working together, we quickly found her to be thoughtful and respectful, and we've always maintained good communication. We've faced many challenges over the years, and Di has always been hands-on in helping us resolve them, which we appreciate. We hold both her and the achievements of the franchise in high regard.

Every business has good times and bad times, and Fernwood is no different. Di has had to navigate a lot of change over the years, and her resilience and perseverance are admirable.

SECRET TO SUCCESS AND LONGEVITY IN BUSINESS

With all the challenges we face running a fitness club, how do we stay motivated and focused? Gin o'clock helps, as does eating cheese every day. That's our secret.

On a more serious note, the key to success and longevity in business and in life is to embrace change. It's all about flexibility – a willingness to change what isn't working and adapt to changing circumstances, such as age or lifestyle. Some habits, such as regular exercise, shouldn't change, but the way we approach them may need to evolve with time. We adapt in ways that best suit our current lifestyles. Staying rigid leads to stagnation, not recreation. While we each have different daily routines, they always focus on faith, family and friends, exercise and nutrition, and sharing life with others.

One belief that has got us through tough times, including recessions and rising interest rates, is: it's quicker to save a dollar than earn a dollar. We always consider the value of every dollar we earn and the effort required to earn it. It's wise to be good stewards of both finance and time.

When times do get tough, we still try to have fun. We communicate our frustrations with each other and vent when necessary. We've also cultivated a lifestyle of fitness in everyday, incidental activities. We enjoy the majority of the things we do but often add in something difficult to build resilience. Of course, we can't always exercise for long periods every day or stick to a rigid routine. Sometimes, we have busy seasons, and our time is limited. So, what do we do? Something. Anything. Ultimately, ten minutes is better than no minutes. Consistency is key. As long as you're doing something consistently, you're still moving forward.

Nicole
HAMBROOK

LIVING AND BREATHING
SPORT AND FITNESS

In 1999, I finished my bachelor's degree in applied science human movements, majoring in exercise management, while working full-time for the Brisbane City Council, managing sports complexes.

In 2002, when I returned from a year in the Netherlands training and supporting my partner, a professional squash player, I decided to use my degree to work as a personal trainer at Fernwood Capalaba. During this time, I was training 50 clients while also working full-time for the council.

Instantly, I fell in love with the women-only environment at Fernwood, and I enjoyed seeing my clients blossom into strong, confident, coordinated women. I loved the environment so much that I decided to purchase my own club, holding the territory of Townsville for 18 months. In July 2006, I went on to purchase the Chermside club and have now spent over two decades with the Fernwood brand.

FINDING THE POSITIVE IN EVERYTHING

Three months after purchasing the Chermside club, a Goodlife gym opened in our shopping centre location, Westfield Chermside. Since then, we've had every new gym franchise or concept open some of their first Brisbane clubs in the same location, with more than 25 competitors within a 5 km radius. Westfield now houses four fitness brands.

I'm a very positive person. To me, the glass is always half full. It's not always easy, but I try to look for a positive in everything. When gym after gym opened in our location, I didn't see it as a threat. Instead, I saw it as an opportunity to up our game and work hard to stay competitive in a saturated market.

MY TRUE PASSIONS

When it comes to our members, my main role is to induct them into the club and ensure they're equipped with the tools to reach their health and fitness goals. I also liaise with physiotherapists, chiropractors, GPs, and surgeons to help members get back to full range, strength, and health post injury or diagnosis. It's something I'm truly passionate about.

I also have an obligation to nurture my staff and help them thrive in their roles. Personally, I treat the cleaner with the same level of respect as I do the CEO, and I believe Di shares this philosophy.

More than anything, I'm passionate about family. Coming from a multigenerational household, with my grandparents living with us, I understand the importance of family and the crucial roles the people in our environments play, whether it be with family, at work, at school, or in sport. Over the years, I've had wonderful role models and countless individuals and moments that have shaped me into the person I am today.

In 2010, I welcomed my son Jake to the world. At age 13, he was Australian champion in discus, while also competing in state championships for cricket and basketball. My greatest joy is watching my beautiful boy explore, excel, and marvel at everything life has to offer. I must admit, having an elite athlete to manage is much like running a business – I need to be hands-on.

LIFE AS I KNOW IT

Coming from a sport background, my training has adapted over the years. At one point, I was training up to five hours a day. That, however, has definitely changed. For the majority of my post-sport life, HIIT-style cardio has served me well. As I head into my later 40s, reformer Pilates is a style of training I've grown to enjoy. While I no longer have time to train five hours a day, I do still train regularly.

As a busy club owner, there always seems to be more to do than what I can fit into my schedule. It can be stressful at times, but to-lists and prioritisation help me tick off the important tasks so I can go to bed at the end of the day content with what I've achieved. I approach each day with an open mind, always aiming to learn something new. In business and in life, we never stop learning.

EVERY SINGLE TIME I'VE FACED A CHALLENGE OR OBSTACLE, *I've overcome* **IT TO EMERGE STRONGER, WISER, MORE PASSIONATE, AND MORE CONFIDENT** *than I was before.*

Lisa-Marie GLEESON

FROM FITNESS HOBBYIST TO FERNWOOD CLUB OWNER

Compared to many others in the network, my journey as a Fernwood franchisee is very new. When I bought the Camberwell club, I felt like I was in a privileged position, as I had worked for the network for over 15 years.

My journey with Fernwood began as a group fitness instructor, and I soon progressed to an in-club coordinator position. Along the way, I studied my Cert IV in Fitness and began personal training. During this time, my boss was a huge role model – in fact, she still is – and she inspired me to want to own a club one day, just like her. At this point, however, it was little more than a dream.

In 2018, the Fernwood support office put out a call for a mum with a baby to volunteer for a postnatal mums and bubs photoshoot. My little Alexander was 9 months old at the time, so I eagerly put my hand up for the job – and I was accepted!

The shoot took place at the Camberwell club, and I vividly recall walking through the doors and immediately thinking, *Wow, what an absolutely gorgeous space.* I took a selfie with Alexander and sent it to my boss with the caption: *I love this club. I want to own this one one day!* Not only did I know I wanted to own a Fernwood club, but now I also knew the exact club I wanted to own. But how would I make it happen?

MAKING MY DREAM A REALITY

In early 2020, soon after the COVID pandemic hit, I took on a club coordinator role at the Camberwell club. My dream job in my dream club – I was a happy girl! I spent the next nine months managing the club virtually while also working with the support office, running virtual, live group fitness classes for the broader Fernwood community, which led to a full-time business development position with the team.

I first met Di in 2018 when she personally presented me with the Fernwood National Kristy Woods Award, a reward given to someone in the network who displays exceptional service to members, fellow workmates, and the Fernwood brand. She was every bit the humble, kind, stylish businesswoman I imagined her to be. Years later, my role in the support office had me working alongside her, and, honestly, it was a 'pinch me' moment every single day. I felt so incredibly lucky to work so closely with such a powerhouse, sharing in her vision for the business.

In the business development role, I developed fitness programs that were delivered to clubs across Australia to be enjoyed by our members, which was both an honour and a privilege. In 2023, I learnt that the Camberwell franchisee was selling the club. Of course, my husband and I jumped at the opportunity – it was a 'now or never' kind of moment. The rest is history!

A SPECIAL SPACE FOR SPECIAL WOMEN

While I had experience supporting other franchisees, nothing could've fully prepared me to captain my own ship. Stepping into a culture of established staff and members was, at times, challenging – I was the new kid on the block, trying to navigate my way through my own business! It took weeks and thousands of questions to understand the business's unique systems and processes. It was stressful and exhausting at times, but the special community and support of the members made the experience much more pleasant and enjoyable. The smiles, energy, thankfulness, and gratefulness of our members make every day absolutely worth it.

For me, the members are by far the best part of running a Fernwood club. Without them, there's no business – they truly are the life and energy between the walls. We laugh together, cry together, sweat together, share in each other's milestones and achievements. It's truly a special privilege to create a space for these incredible people.

The most wonderful and special thing about my club is that it's over 20 years old. We have many mums who were members of the gym before it even became a Fernwood. Some women who would leave their kids in the creche while they worked out now train in the club *with* their daughters. It's truly special to know that these ladies are sharing their health and fitness journey in this space with their daughters, paving a path for them to follow.

MY CLUB OWNER SURVIVAL GUIDE

As a busy club owner, kicking off the day with exercise is key for me. It sets me up to navigate the day with a clear mind and an abundance of energy. Most mornings, I'm up at 5:30 am, getting a workout in before our family's morning routine begins.

Meal prep is also extremely important. As a business owner, the days are often long, and a lack of meal prep can lead to a lot of bought lunches and takeaway dinners. I do one big grocery shop every Sunday, and my dinners are all planned before the week begins. This ensures healthy meals all throughout the week.

The first thing I do when I get to work each morning is set clear goals and priorities for the day ahead. This helps me stay focused on the most important tasks and ensures that I make progress towards my objectives. If there are larger projects to work on, I break them down into smaller, manageable tasks, allowing me to tackle them one at a time while maintaining a sense of accomplishment. When I can, I also like to participate in some group fitness classes during the day. This breaks up the work and helps me maintain productivity and prevent burnout.

I also have a dedicated workspace for myself in the club that's free from interruptions and unnecessary clutter. This helps me stay fully engaged in my work and minimises the chances of getting sidetracked. I've found that the many little things you do to make your life easier can add up to a big difference.

FAILURE IS A STEPPING STONE

Over the years, my life has taken many twists and turns; however, having children created one of the biggest changes in my life. Before kids, my career was in interior design. Group Fitness was a hobby of sorts, which I fulfilled before and after work. My first two babies were born within 16 months of each other, and the flexibility of teaching group fitness was extremely convenient and meant I could keep working while being a busy mum.

During this time, my passion for fitness really blossomed. My work hours increased as the kids got older, and I never went back to interior design, continuing along the path from fitness hobbyist to Fernwood club owner.

On my journey, the motto "failure is a stepping stone to success" is something I've reminded myself of every day, and it has rung true in so many situations in both my career and personal life. Every single time I've faced a challenge or obstacle, I've overcome it to emerge stronger, wiser, more passionate, and more confident than I was before. The difficult moments are opportunities to grow as a person and as a business. While you may not immediately see the light at the end of the tunnel, that tunnel always leads to better days. It's a truth I live by every day.

I'VE ALWAYS BELIEVED IN PUTTING *others first* AND TREATING THEM WITH RESPECT, WITH *the hope that* THEY'LL TREAT ME AND OTHERS THE SAME.

Melinda
WILSON

PUTTING OUR MEMBERS FIRST

My introduction to health and fitness came from my grand-mother. She was someone I always looked up to. She never drove a car and instead chose to walk everywhere she went. She even bought a top-floor unit so she could walk the stairs every day. My grandmother never smoked, never drank alcohol, and her diet was full of fruit, vegetables, fish, and all the right things to help her body stay strong. The constant exercise kept her fit and healthy, and she maintained a good weight all throughout her life and never looked tired. My beautiful grandmother lived to be 94 years old, dying of natural causes.

Another wonderful lady I took inspiration from was my husband's aunt, who was diagnosed with breast cancer and never gave up fighting, always believing she would beat it.

Aunty still exercised while receiving her treatment, knowing it would help keep her body strong to fight her illness.

Both of these extraordinary women taught me the value of staying physically active regardless of age or circumstances. So, in 2019, when the opportunity arose to take on a Fernwood Fitness club, my husband Talbot and I decided to go for it.

Unfortunately, a year after, the 2020 COVID pandemic hit Australia, and we were forced to permanently close our doors. Having to tell our staff and members that the club would no longer be there was tough, and many tears were shed.

During this time, I learnt that it's best to keep emotions out of business decisions. When something goes wrong, it's important to take a step back and get your emotions in check so you can make the best, most logical decisions for you and your business. When COVID closed down our first club, my emotional response was to decide it was far too risky to start another one with everything going on in the world and after everything we had lost. It was one of the most stressful times of our lives, but we persevered and opened our new club just 12 months later, coming back stronger than ever.

THE FLAWLESS FERNWOOD MODEL

The fact that Fernwood is all about women's health is a big drawcard. With the worst of the pandemic behind us, we went on to grow our new club's member base to over 1800 beautiful ladies. I love hearing how Fernwood offers these women an environment where they feel safe and comfortable to exercise. Some of our members see Fernwood as their second home, being able to sit and relax in the members' lounge when they finish exercising, while having beautiful bathrooms and everything else available to them.

It gives us great satisfaction to be able to provide the ladies of our area with a clean, safe environment to exercise in and access to staff who are fully dedicated to women's health and fitness. Our wonderful staff are like a second family to these ladies, listening when they need to talk and guiding them to achieve healthy lifestyles. We get great satisfaction from seeing the transformation of our members and watching them meet, and even exceed, their fitness goals. The in-club challenges we run give the ladies some friendly competition while pushing them to be fitter and stronger. We have a wide range of ages in our club, with some of the older ladies giving the young girls a run for their money in our dedicated small group fitness classes. How inspiring these older women are – I'm constantly in awe of their dedication to their health.

Talbot and I love the Fernwood model so much that we've decided to open a second club to help more ladies with their fitness journeys.

A WONDERFUL OPPORTUNITY

Owning a Fernwood Fitness has changed our lifestyle, allow-ing us to spend more time with family and facilitating our daughter's own fitness journey.

I'm extremely fortunate to own a Fernwood Fitness club where I can go in any day of the week and do a workout. It helps me stay fit, even when life gets busy. Most mornings, I work out in the club before Talbot and I grab a cuppa and plan for the day ahead. We also try to walk in the mornings to change up the scenery and give us more time to chat about how we can improve the club and our members' experience. We're always looking to offer more value for money. For example, we've added child minding and infrared sauna to our memberships at no additional cost. To us, giving our ladies great value for money is important.

I've always believed in putting others first and treating them with respect, with the hope that they'll treat me and others the same. As a club owner, I now have the opportunity to put the ladies in our community first and give them a place to feel respected and valued. It's a wonderful feeling, and I wouldn't have it any other way.

Janet
SALTARELLI

LOVE AT FIRST SIGHT

When my husband Angelo and I decided we wanted to start a family business, I was working at Fernwood Sydenham as the personal training coordinator. We explored a variety of franchise opportunities around Melbourne, but we couldn't find a business venture that resonated with us.

Soon, I heard that several Fernwood clubs were on the market. Perfect! By the time we walked through the doors of Fernwood Carlton, we had already looked at several other clubs, but none had caught our attention. However, as soon as I entered the Carlton club, I fell in love. "This is the one," I said to Angelo, and he agreed. I felt an overwhelming sense of joy and couldn't wait to tell our girls that we were going to make an offer to buy a Fernwood.

On Valentine's Day 2014, the previous club owner accepted

our offer. On 15 May the same year, we became the proud Franchisee owners of Fernwood Carlton.

A POWERFUL SUPPORT NETWORK

I'm fortunate to come from a loving family that supports me on my journey. They've shaped me into the person I am today. When I was a little girl, my mum said to me, "Treat others the way you want to be treated yourself," and that's exactly what I do. I'm always honest, compassionate, understanding, and I treat everyone with the respect they deserve.

I'm also incredibly fortunate to work alongside my husband and our two beautiful daughters, Lauren and Madison. It really is a family business, and we wouldn't have it any other way.

I must admit, there is one downside to all of us working in the club: separating work from home can be difficult. It only takes one family member to mention Fernwood for the four of us to all start talking about work. However, we've tried to simplify maintaining a good work-life balance. The solution? When we physically leave the club, it's time to 'log off' and enjoy time outside of Fernwood.

I've now been the franchisee owner of Fernwood Carlton for almost a decade, and I've definitely matured over the years, learning to stand up for myself and what I believe in. Understanding the day-to-day running of a business has been a steep learning curve, and I now understand that you can never really be ready for the challenges and surprises you encounter along the way. In my case, having a support network of franchisees has been vital. As a Fernwood club owner, you don't have to do it alone. Other franchisees have already experienced many of the issues you'll face, and their support is invaluable. A couple of franchisees have become my Fernie best friends, and I chat with them nearly every day. They're my rock, my cheer squad, my support network. They pick me up when I need it and always encourage me to be the best version of myself.

THE INSPIRING WOMEN IN MY LIFE

Every day, our members inspire and uplift me. I love seeing them succeed and become the best versions of themselves. Although I could write a whole book praising our members, I want to give a shout-out to a handful of particularly inspiring women.

- **Anna** – At our 2023 Christmas party, over a few drinks, I was chatting to Anna about needing additional cycle instructors, as I wanted to add extra classes to the club timetable. Anna said she wanted to help and offered to attend an 8-week training course to become a cycle instructor. She is now a qualified Les Mills RPM instructor and an asset to our Fernie family. The members adore her.

- **Pat** – Pat just had her 70th birthday (I hope she doesn't mind me announcing this to the world), but you wouldn't know it. She's an absolute legend who can leg press 180 kg. In our personal training sessions, we often chat about how age is just a number. Never let your age define who you are or what you can lift. She's an inspiration to all women.

- **Marie** – I've trained Marie for 15 years. Six years ago, she was advised she needed to have a full knee replacement. However, personal training sessions, focusing on strength, and guided rehabilitation from her physiotherapist have helped her delay surgery. She has an incredible determination to postpone the day she will need the operation, and she even completes her rehab exercises when she's on holiday.

- **Nichole** – Nichole trains with us every day, sometimes twice a day. We love her enthusiasm and bubbly personality. Recently, we were so happy to hear that, with the guidance of her doctor, she has been able to reduce her medication.

It's not only our members who inspire me but our staff too. I have an amazing team of women who support me with the day-to-day running of the club – they're my Fernie family! All my staff work tirelessly to promote the brand, help women join with the membership that's best for them, and support our members on every step of their health and wellness journeys. I've always advised my staff to be honest when selling a membership. The goal is to sell with integrity and to never sell a membership if they think the prospect doesn't understand what's been said. It's the first step in building a relationship based on trust. We want our members to trust us with their health journeys, and, of course, we want to help them succeed.

Some days in the club are tough, so I believe it's so important that, as a team, we get to celebrate all our wins, big and small, along with our birthdays – always with cake!

At the end of the day, my life is richer because all the women I've mentioned – members, staff, and other franchisees – are a part of it.

ALWAYS CHALLENGE YOURSELF

At my very first Fernwood conference, Di asked me what I was going to implement when I got back to the club. "Everything," I replied. Her wise response was to focus on one thing at a time, which is something I've done ever since. You can't do it all at once. You can only move forward one step at a time.

Business is always changing, and, if you want to stay at the forefront of the fitness industry, you must move with the times. This might mean furthering your studies, working on your self-development, or implementing a new Fernwood program in club. It's important to keep challenging yourself and to continue to grow as a person and a business owner.

My life motto has always been: one door closes, and another one opens. Life is a journey. Yes, you will make mistakes, and sometimes things won't go according to your big master plan, but that's okay, as long as you learn from your setbacks. When one door closes and you think it's the end of the world, it's not, because another door is opening, and what's behind it will be bigger and better than anything you could've imagined.

I BELIEVE WE HAVE *one purpose* IN LIFE, AND THAT PURPOSE IS TO GIVE.

Binish
MOBEEN

— MELTON, VICTORIA —

APPROACHING BUSINESS WITH A SERVICE MENTALITY

Before coming to Australia, my husband Mobin and I had a couple of franchises in the telecom sector. When choosing a franchise, we understand the value of going with a reputable and well-run organisation to ensure the business runs smoothly. For our latest venture, we wanted to combine business with one of our interests, something we loved. Essentially, we wanted to enjoy ourselves while we made a living.

Both Mobin and I are into fitness, and we understand the importance of exercise when it comes to achieving good mental and physical health. In fact, we believe that exercise is a necessity, not a luxury. Fitness is a lifelong commitment.

When we discovered Fernwood, we knew we had stumbled upon something special. We loved the idea of a women-only facility where members could feel comfortable and secure, especially from a religious and cultural perspective. We both agreed that we had found our next franchise, and, after meeting Di, who was very warm and welcoming, we became the owners of Fernwood Melton.

SPEAKING OUR MEMBERS' LANGUAGE

While Melton was a growing suburb, it came with a unique challenge. It has a high obesity rate compared to many other areas, so selling the idea of being fit and healthy was difficult.

To boost sales and retain members, we had to learn marketing and selling strategies that resonated with the Melton demographic. Not all clubs use the same strategies, and we had to learn what made the women in our community tick.

To get the message across, we used social media, posting pictures and videos that showed what it's like to work out in a women-only environment, free of judgement but full of encouragement. We also did a lot of local marketing, which included in-club and over-the-phone consultations.

While many women are reluctant to join the club, once they do, their attitude completely changes, and they don't like to miss a day! So many of our members have improved themselves both mentally and physically in our club – it's truly inspirational.

MY ROLE AS A LEADER

For me, owning a club presented several challenges. Firstly, as an introvert, I struggled to mingle with members and staff. However, over time, I learnt to come out of my shell and do what was necessary to support the club.

As a leader, it's my job to make our members and staff feel comfortable, safe, and secure. It's not all about profit or personal gain for me. Our members and staff come first. Understanding this has made me a good team player, who's always empathetic to our staff and members.

With that said, finding the right staff can be challenging. Now, when hiring, I look for someone who has the right attitude, aligns with our purpose, wants to empower women, and has a genuine interest in growing the club. To ensure we get the right people, I strictly screen all candidates throughout the hiring process.

Once you have the right staff, it's important to keep up with their training so they're always learning, growing, and improving in their roles. Keeping your team both educated and motivated is crucial to the success of your business.

ONE PURPOSE IN LIFE

As a busy club owner, I almost never take days off during the week. However, if life happens, I'm fortunate that I can take time off if needed. It's the beauty of being in this business!

For me, exercise is a top priority, and I get up early each day to ensure I never miss a session. I also like to regularly take some time for myself to step back and examine the bigger picture. When you're constantly caught up in the day-to-day running of a business, it's easy to lose sight of your overall vision.

Ultimately, I approach my role as a Fernwood club owner with a service mentality. Serving our members is my priority. I love that I get to meet women from all walks of life, listen to their stories, and learn about their unique experiences and achievements.

I believe we have one purpose in life, and that purpose is to give. It's a belief that influences everything I do both personally and professionally.

Filipa
FERREIRA

DETERMINED TO SUCCEED

At 16 years old, I moved in with my grandparents, 300 km away from the rest of my family in Lisbon. It was a difficult time, but I believe it was the catalyst for me developing an unwavering determination to succeed at everything I do.

At age 23, I married the man of my dreams, but that didn't mean my struggles were over. My marriage came with a condition: I had to move from Portugal to Australia. The first two years were horrendously difficult. Suddenly, I was thrust into a completely foreign culture, trying to speak a language I didn't fully understand. I was very lonely.

For several years, I worked in my father in law's businesses, gaining management experience and confidence in my ability to navigate my new country of residence. At age 28, I started a bookkeeping business, but I didn't stop there. At age 32, I decided to add an energy auditing business while continuing to grow my bookkeeping business. I was determined to succeed in life, and things were looking good – until the global financial crisis (GFC) hit, and we lost everything.

When the GFC rocked the world, our businesses couldn't withstand the shock, and we lost not only them but also our house, our investment properties, the lot. All we could do was learn from the experience, keep pushing forward, and begin the process of rebuilding our lives.

A BREATH OF LIFE

In 2013, I started working as a personal trainer at Fernwood Fitness Miranda. For years on the job, I daydreamed of taking over the club and breathing new life into it. When the opportunity finally arose, I grabbed hold of it with both hands.

Buying Fernwood Miranda was like buying a corpse. A lot of the equipment needed to be repaired or replaced, and the whole club needed a fresh coat of paint. Over time, members had lost faith in the business, but I was determined to give it some serious CPR and bring it back to life.

My family and I spent almost two years painting the club and replacing equipment, using every available dollar to transform it into a more vibrant and welcoming space. We spent every minute of every weekend and public holiday in the club, cleaning, painting, moving equipment, creating the space I dreamed our members should have for entrusting us with their journeys. Finally, the transformation was complete, and it was time to get out and start marketing.

KEEP PUSHING FORWARD

In the end, our hard work paid off, and we now run a beautiful and vibrant club. What I love most about running a Fernwood club is having the ability to change lives. We inspire people to do more and be more, creating a positive impact in the community. For me, that's the best reward anyone could ask for.

I absolutely love what I do, and I love being in the club. Sure, sometimes running a business can get overwhelming, but I've learnt to take some downtime when I need it. I also exercise every day, either by teaching classes or participating myself. With everything I do, I always add a personal touch. It's something that has helped make my club so successful.

All of my life experiences have taught me that no matter what happens, if you keep going, life does get better. Tomorrow is another day, so, if you're struggling today, keep pushing forward – it will get easier.

IN LIFE, THERE
ARE ALWAYS
CHALLENGES.
YOU CAN EITHER
LET THEM PULL YOU
DOWN OR USE THEM
TO CLIMB TO
greater heights.

Kathie
LONG

WHEN YOU LOVE WHAT YOU DO

When I decided to become a Fernwood franchisee, I had arrived at a point in my life where it was time to embrace some changes and look for new opportunities. I had spent decades in roles that focused on helping others. I knew I loved helping people, being healthy, and helping women to see their infinite worth. I knew it was now time to bring together all of my knowledge, values, strengths, and marketable skills.

This transitional time in my life coincided with my husband, Colin, being diagnosed with a rare eye condition that meant we needed to create a different lifestyle for our family. Up until this point, Colin had been in very demanding jobs. While he thoroughly enjoyed the challenge, the stress was taking a toll on his health and wellbeing. Then we found our Fernwood.

From the moment I walked into the club, I loved it! It was the opportunity we had been looking for, and I could see that this was a place where I could use all of my acquired skills and continue to grow both personally and professionally.

When we first came into our club, we had a lot to learn, and we both thrived on the challenge. With our amazing team, we steadily grew our membership base. We loved building our team of women who loved learning and bringing their professional best and great care for others into our Fernwood community. In life, there are always challenges. You can either let them pull you down or use them to climb to greater heights.

AN UNFORTUNATE ACCIDENT

In 2019, on a Friday night after work, I was walking down the front steps of my house when I missed the bottom step, resulting in a dislocated and broken ankle and a broken leg.

After going to the hospital and being examined, I asked the surgeon on call that night, "So, if I have surgery tonight, will I be back at work Monday?" I followed up with, "And will I be able to wear high heels once I've recovered?" The surgeon advised me that I wouldn't be back at work two days after surgery – not even close. However, he softened the blow by letting me know I would be able to wear high heels again. Yay!

Right before my accident, one of my key team members had left for annual leave. When I explained what had happened, her response was an instant: "Would you like me to turn back and cancel my holiday?" This is the calibre of women I'm fortunate to have in my life. They're amazing. Our amazing team pulled together, and there was no need for anyone to cancel their holidays.

I spent the next six weeks in bed, leg elevated, non-weight-bearing, which meant I wasn't able to be with my members or my team. During this time, my team did an amazing job of looking after our business and me. Members sent cards and well wishes, and my team visited me and sent Colin home with care packages on a regular basis. One of the beautiful head office team members sent me a care package as well. I'll be forever grateful for the wonderful community I'm a part of.

While I was recovering, I worked from home on marketing and promotions, holding more than one meeting from my bed. My team, knowing me, would send work home with Colin, along with workouts designed for my recovery.

Through our team pulling together, we overcame this challenge, and it wasn't long before I was back in the club where I thrive. Challenges were not new to us, and, as a team and personally, we had experience in becoming stronger together.

RISING TO THE CHALLENGE

Within weeks of purchasing our club, we learnt that Colin had an eye condition that could cost him his eyesight, and he had to stop working and driving immediately. His diagnosis was devastating news, and it meant we needed to change the way we worked.

Rising up and facing the challenge together, we determined our new roles in life and did what needed to be done. It was a pivotal moment for us, our family, and our team.

Thankfully, Colin is now able to drive again, and his skills keep all of our equipment running smoothly. Our Fernwood also gives Colin the continued opportunity to work in a project management role, which he loves.

I'm extremely proud of the way our family and our team rose to the challenge of Colin's eye condition, and I'm grateful for our strong team members, who have stood with us and supported us by bringing their very best every day. With each challenge we face, we only grow stronger.

PRACTICALLY SPEECHLESS...

Over the years, we've had many amusing moments in our club. However, one story in particular sticks out in my mind.

Colin was completing some work in our downstairs bathrooms, and he had gone to a lot of trouble to close them off with witch's hats, 'do not enter' police-style tape, 'maintenance in progress' signs, and signs directing members to our amenities upstairs. To make the downstairs bathrooms even more inaccessible, he had placed chairs to block the bathroom entrances.

I was in reception when Colin came out of the bathrooms looking shaky and a bit pale. After somewhat regaining his composure, he explained what had happened. One of our more mature members found her way through all of the blockades and entered the change room portion of the bathroom. Colin heard a noise and went to investigate. He found the member putting her belongings in a locker and when he explained that he had closed the downstairs bathrooms to complete some work and asked if she could use the change room upstairs, she gave him a cheeky wink and said, "I don't want to walk upstairs. You won't peek, will you?" At this, Colin fled the area as fast as he could, learning that you can't keep a determined woman from her mission.

EMPOWERING MYSELF AND OTHERS TO SHINE

Living a healthy lifestyle full of movement and good nutrition is important to me, as it's an investment in my health and future. While finding time to exercise regularly can be challenging, it has always been a priority. When I'm disciplined and healthy, it helps me to bring my best to my members, my team, my family, and the Fernwood network. I'll admit, it's convenient that I have a very short commute from my office to the gym – it's right through the door – so I don't have any excuses. I work out most days and even through injury, I kept moving, focusing on consistency, rehabilitation, and doing the best I could manage at the time.

My daily routine involves more than just movement and work. Generally, I start the day with some quiet time, reading devotions, reading my bible, and setting my intention for the day. At the end of each day, I write my to-do list for tomorrow. Once this is done, I put my phone away, unwind, and practise the same quiet-time routine as the morning. I also spend some time reflecting on the day that was (what I could improve and what went well). I finish my night with non-business reading and as I close my eyes, I focus on the top three things I'm thankful for from the day.

I also have a yearly tradition. Each year, I choose a word or phrase to focus on. In 2024, my word is 'design'. The year is all about designing my hours, days, weeks, and months to be in alignment with my values. When you love what you do for work, it's easy to end up doing too much, and I find that having a focus for the year is important for maintaining a good work-life balance.

The thing is, I really do love what I do. Colin and I feel deeply blessed to be a part of an organisation that believes in empowering women to shine and aims to help them improve their lives every day and in every way.

THROUGH THE
STRENGTH OF
FRANCHISING,
FERNWOOD HAS
ignited the flame
IN SO MANY WOMEN
WHO MAY NOT HAVE
GONE DOWN
the path of being
BUSINESS WOMEN
IF IT WERE NOT FOR
FERNWOOD.

WHEN WOMEN SEE
OTHER WOMEN
breaking
barriers
AND THRIVING
IN THE INDUSTRY,
IT ENCOURAGES
THEM
to pursue
THEIR OWN
ENTREPRENEURIAL
DREAMS.

Some Final Words From
DIANA WILLIAMS

Female entrepreneurs have been making significant strides in many industries, including the health and fitness industry, bringing fresh perspectives, innovative ideas, and a keen understanding of consumer needs.

As women, we often recognise a gap in the market and are not afraid to think outside the box to create products that resonate with women's unique requirements. As more women take on leadership roles in health and fitness companies, they become role models for others to follow. Representation matters, and seeing successful women in these positions inspires others to follow suit.

Since I started Fernwood 35 years ago, I have seen a gradual rise in the number of female leaders in our industry. The more there are, the more role models we have.

I hope that you've enjoyed reading the stories of these amazing women, their backgrounds, and their goals, and I hope that having read them you feel empowered to embark on a journey of your own to discover new skills you never thought you had. Or maybe you knew you had the skills but not the courage to utilise them.

You are strong, intelligent, and savvy. Have the confidence to follow your dreams, set yourself realistic goals, and start out on the journey – just one little step at a time. If someone had told me 40 years ago that I would be the founder and managing director of an iconic national brand, I would have laughed out loud. But my journey started with just one little step – by opening up a tiny place for women to work out. The reality is, I landed where I am today, 35 years later. You don't know what you are capable of unless you start. Starting is the hardest part – then you're off and running, and you will be amazed at how far it takes you. You will make mistakes along the way; you will have days when you wonder what on earth you were thinking, but then you will have other wonderful days of pride, self-belief, and recognising all that you have achieved. You too can become a role model to other women and young girls, showing them that if they follow their dreams, anything is possible – the only thing standing in their way is themselves.

When women see other women breaking barriers and thriving in the industry, it encourages them to pursue their own entrepreneurial dreams. Women understand women. Female entrepreneurs can tap into their firsthand experiences and insights to create products and services that cater specifically to women's health and fitness needs. Whether it's wellness apps, activewear, or fitness programs, women-led businesses can tailor their offerings to address the unique challenges and preferences of women.

As women, we often take a holistic approach to health and wellness. We recognise that physical fitness is just one aspect of overall wellbeing. We are driving the trend toward integrated wellness solutions that combine nutrition, mental health, and self-care.

Historically, the health and fitness industry has been male-dominated. However, as women, we are challenging these stereotypes and proving that we can lead and succeed.

As more women step into leadership roles, we can expect continued innovation and a positive change in our industry. Women are no longer just participating; we are leading the way.

Di William

Connect
WITH US

To connect with us and access bonus content and exclusive offers, scan the QR code or follow the link. We look forward to sharing more with you.

SCAN ME

www.fernwoodfitness.com.au/womenfittolead

www.ingramcontent.com/pod-product-compliance
Lightning Source LLC
Chambersburg PA
CBHW052111030426
42335CB00025B/2941